"Just as Lea's mother handed her a book on highly sensitive people (HSPs), Lea has handed teens a book uniquely their own. Lea's compassionate voice encourages the teen, provides understanding and practical tips, but above all, lets them know they are not alone."

—Susie Click, LPC, private practice therapist

"With *The Highly Sensitive Teen*, Lea Noring balances big-picture, accessible explanations that help teens understand their sensitive reactions to the world around them with specific strategies for managing the challenges that come with that sensitivity. This will be a go-to therapist recommendation for adolescent clients as well as their parents."

—Taylor Trussell, licensed professional counselor

"This is the book we've been waiting for! Cover to cover, Lea Noring gifts us with her warmth and wisdom. Brimming with stories, resources, and tips for everyday living, *The Highly Sensitive Teen* transcends how to survive and prepares readers to thrive."

—Lisa Hedden, PhD, LPC, counselor educator, and owner of Footpath Partners counseling practice in Atlanta, GA

"I highly endorse *The Highly Sensitive Teen* as a valuable resource for teens and their families. It offers insightful facts, self-assessments, and practical tools to help teens manage emotional intensity and overstimulation—fostering resilience and growth. This book also encourages healthy relationships and personal development, making it a must-read for understanding and supporting highly sensitive teens. I look forward to introducing it to our students, offering positive solutions for neurodiverse children."

—Lisa Mitchell, CEO of Everything Under The ~~~ ~~
substance use disorder specialist f
children, autism, dyslexia, and em

T0273512

the *instant* help
solutions series

Young people today need mental health resources more than ever. That's why New Harbinger created the **Instant Help Solutions Series** especially for teens. Written by leading psychologists, physicians, and professionals, these evidence-based self-help books offer practical tips and strategies for dealing with a variety of mental health issues and life challenges teens face, such as depression, anxiety, bullying, eating disorders, trauma, and self-esteem problems.

Studies have shown that young people who learn healthy coping skills early on are better able to navigate problems later in life. Engaging and easy-to-use, these books provide teens with the tools they need to thrive—at home, at school, and on into adulthood.

This series is part of the **New Harbinger Instant Help Books** imprint, founded by renowned child psychologist Lawrence Shapiro. For a complete list of books in this series, visit newharbinger.com.

THE
HIGHLY
SENSITIVE
TEEN

Using Your Hidden Powers to
Balance Emotions, Set Boundaries,
and Embrace Who You Are

LEA NORING, PHD

Instant Help Books
An Imprint of New Harbinger Publications, Inc.

Publisher's Note

This publication is designed to provide accurate and authoritative information in regard to the subject matter covered. It is sold with the understanding that the publisher is not engaged in rendering psychological, financial, legal, or other professional services. If expert assistance or counseling is needed, the services of a competent professional should be sought.

INSTANT HELP, the Clock Logo, and NEW HARBINGER are trademarks of New Harbinger Publications, Inc.

New Harbinger Publications is an employee-owned company.

Copyright © 2025 by Lea Noring
Instant Help Books
An imprint of New Harbinger Publications, Inc.
5720 Shattuck Avenue
Oakland, CA 94609
www.newharbinger.com

Cover design by Sara Christian

Acquired by Jess O'Brien

Edited by Karen Schader

Library of Congress Cataloging-in-Publication Data on file

NCEO MEMBER
NATIONAL CENTER FOR EMPLOYEE OWNERSHIP

FSC
www.fsc.org

MIX
Paper | Supporting responsible forestry
FSC® C008955

Printed in the United States of America

27   26   25

10   9   8   7   6   5   4   3   2   1   First Printing

CONTENTS

FOREWORD

Teen brains are—quite literally—wired to be sensitive. Without going into a complicated biology lesson, teen brains are still under construction. According to neuroscience, the average teen brain has an extremely active amygdala, which is the part of the brain that can lead teens to experience things as "dangerous" even when everything is actually safe and okay.

So, every teenager in the world is sensitive.

But if you're reading this book, chances are you (or the teen in your life) were sensitive long before becoming a teenager. It's also likely that you're much more sensitive than many of your peers.

Throughout your life, you have probably heard that you are "too much" in many different ways—too sensitive to criticism, too uncomfortable in new settings or around new people, too reactive when things don't go your way, too caring or emotional or irritable or shy or...you can fill in the blank better than I can.

And it gets really confusing because you're getting this "too much" message from people who know you and love you and are trying to help. But because they (and you) do not understand highly sensitive people (HSP), it turns out that sometimes, it's not very helpful.

If you think you might be an HSP, this book can help you a lot! Lea is going to do three things for you:

- First, she's going to help you understand what it means to be an HSP (highly sensitive person) and guide you to let go of the belief that you're "too much" of anything!

- Next, as you understand yourself better, she'll help you educate those close to you about what are, for you, very reasonable needs.

- Finally, she'll help you learn to take care of yourself, set appropriate boundaries without offending others, and lean into the gifts of being an HSP.

Yes, I said gifts. As someone who is kind of an expert on all things neurospicy, I get that sometimes it can be a pain in the neck being an HSP. I also know, with 1000-percent certainty, that once you get a handle on it, it can bring spectacular gifts to your life!

With awareness and acceptance of your unique sensitivities, you will experience more joy and fulfillment in life.

At this moment, it's possible that your extremely active amygdala is sending you false messages. Maybe it's telling you that joy and fulfillment are "too much" to expect from reading a book, or that being an HSP is really not that important to the rest of your life.

But that's simply not true. Here's a little secret that adults don't like to admit: most adults struggle with self-acceptance. In fact, adults tend to have at least one nagging, self-critical voice in their head. And more often than not, they started listening to that voice when they were teenagers.

So, I encourage you to curl up in a really comfy place and give yourself permission to take yourself seriously. Because understanding yourself as an HSP can set the stage for how you think about yourself...for the rest of your life.

—Elaine Taylor-Klaus, MCC
ImpactParents.com
Author of *The Essential Guide to Raising Complex Kids with ADHD, Anxiety and More*

INTRODUCTION

Sensitivity can be a sensitive subject.

It is for me, and I'll tell you why. I can remember being in preschool and the teacher telling my mother, "She's oversensitive." That message was repeated in parent-teacher conferences and on my grade reports all the way through to my high school graduation.

"You're too sensitive to live in this world," an exasperated friend once told me after I was deeply bothered by a television series about embarrassing pranks played on unsuspecting people.

But actually, I am not too sensitive to live in this world, and neither are you! The world benefits from the highly sensitive viewpoint and would be a place of lesser beauty without it. So often, teens are just beginning to discover their sensitivity and don't realize that they make the world more beautiful just by being their authentic selves. That's why I said yes to the opportunity to write this book for you.

I've noticed that sensitive people are sometimes told "Toughen up!" and "Suck it up, buttercup." Toughening up is not what I want to talk to you about. I want to talk to you about what's going on when you feel uncomfortable and what to do about it. Self-understanding helps build both self-esteem and self-respect.

When Dr. Elaine Aron's first edition of *The Highly Sensitive Person* was published in 1996, my mother startled me one afternoon by presenting it to me immediately when I walked through her front door.

"Here!" she said. "I think you need this."

I glanced at the title on the cover. Highly sensitive, huh? It sounded like it might be a fit.

That night I curled up on the sofa and started reading. I read about characteristics like having a deep and rich inner life full of interesting thoughts and intriguing daydreams. I read about being deeply affected by music and art, and I thought about how I was sometimes moved to tears by music and art and sometimes moved to agitation and aversion. Dr. Aron was onto something huge, and I knew her book would change lives.

Now that *The Highly Sensitive Person* is in its twenty-fifth anniversary edition (Aron 2020) and more than seventy books about highly sensitive people (HSPs) have been published, not only have lives been changed but the way society sees sensitivity has started to change. I think we now understand that many people are strongly empathetic. Teachers now know what to do when students have sensory issues in the classroom. This may be because we talk more these days about personality type, temperament, and different types of brain wiring, such as ADHD and autism. And I think the idea of the HSP and the way it has caught on is a big part of that positive change.

This book is designed for you, so you'll know what high sensitivity is and what it means to be an HSP. It's a hands-on practical guidebook to help you with challenges like explaining high sensitivity to parents, teachers, and friends. You'll find questions to reflect on; if you like, you can use your journal to reply to those. You'll also find some lists that ask you to select terms that apply to you; those lists can be downloaded at http://www. newharbinger.com/54032. At the end of the book, you'll find encouraging affirmations; you can download those and keep them in an easily available spot so you can say them to yourself often.

We'll also talk about how to handle criticism, how to be as comfortable as possible on an overnight trip, how to handle friend drama, and how to feel better on a very bad day when it seems like the world is against you.

With all the books about HSPs, do we really need one for teens? I'd say we probably need five or six. Teens like you, gifted with the trait of high sensitivity, need encouragement and guidance as you try to figure out how the world works and what your place in it is.

CHAPTER 1

ARE YOU HIGHLY SENSITIVE?

"You're too sensitive!" Do you hear this a lot? If so, you may be sensitive, but not *too* sensitive. Being sensitive is not a bad thing, and it doesn't mean you need to change to be tougher or to be anyone other than who you are.

What being highly sensitive does mean is being very aware of what is happening around and within you—harsh words, loud noises, bright lights, sad music, strong smells, uncomfortable seats. Things like this might be overwhelming and affect you more than they would someone else. And that's okay! The world needs highly sensitive people to notice when the atmosphere has gotten too negative or too intense.

There are actually a lot of people who are sensitive that way—you're not alone. Psychologist and sensitivity expert Dr. Elaine Aron (2023) has stated that 15 to 20 percent of people could be considered highly sensitive, so that means there are a lot of others who experience life the way you do.

Is there a way to know for sure if you're not just sensitive but *highly* sensitive? Yes! Read on for a short quiz that is also available for downloading at http://www.newharbinger.com/54032.

High Sensitivity Indicator Quiz

For each statement, circle the statement that sounds most like you.

Loud noises make me uncomfortable.

Sounds like me • A little like me • Maybe, maybe not like me • Not really like me

I need my environment to smell nice.

Sounds like me • A little like me • Maybe, maybe not like me • Not really like me

People sometimes think I'm shy.

Sounds like me • A little like me • Maybe, maybe not like me • Not really like me

I easily notice small changes in my environment.

Sounds like me • A little like me • Maybe, maybe not like me • Not really like me

I don't like to be around people who are arguing.

Sounds like me • A little like me • Maybe, maybe not like me • Not really like me

It can bother me a lot when I feel people are watching me.

Sounds like me • A little like me • Maybe, maybe not like me • Not really like me

I don't like to have a lot of stuff going on at once.

Sounds like me • A little like me • Maybe, maybe not like me • Not really like me

I get startled easily by sudden sounds or sudden movements.

Sounds like me • A little like me • Maybe, maybe not like me • Not really like me

I am deeply moved by beautiful music and beautiful art.

Sounds like me • A little like me • Maybe, maybe not like me • Not really like me

I can't watch shows with a lot of violence.

Sounds like me • A little like me • Maybe, maybe not like me • Not really like me

My feelings can get hurt when people are harsh or critical.

Sounds like me • A little like me • Maybe, maybe not like me • Not really like me

I can tell when other people are upset, even if they try to hide it.

Sounds like me • A little like me • Maybe, maybe not like me • Not really like me ·

I dislike bright, glaring lights more than most of my friends do.

Sounds like me • A little like me • Maybe, maybe not like me • Not really like me

I seem to feel emotions more deeply than other people.

Sounds like me • A little like me • Maybe, maybe not like me • Not really like me

I need more downtime and alone time than most of my friends do.

Sounds like me • A little like me • Maybe, maybe not like me • Not really like me

It can take me a while to make a final decision on things.

Sounds like me • A little like me • Maybe, maybe not like me • Not really like me

Hectic environments bother me.

Sounds like me • A little like me • Maybe, maybe not like me • Not really like me

Strong flavors, textures, and smells in food are often too much for me.

Sounds like me • *A little like me* • *Maybe, maybe not like me* • *Not really like me*

If I'm not given time to prepare, change in routine or environment can make me anxious.

Sounds like me • *A little like me* • *Maybe, maybe not like me* • *Not really like me*

Scoring:

Give yourself 7 points for every "Sounds like me."

Give yourself 4 points for every "A little like me."

Give yourself 1 point for every "Maybe, maybe not like me."

Give yourself 0 points for every "Not really like me."

If you get 95 points or higher, you are probably a highly sensitive person (HSP).

You may be thinking *So I am a highly sensitive person! What do I do now?*

You don't actually have to do anything, but it would be good to pause and get more comfortable with the idea of being an HSP.

When Emily, age fourteen, took the quiz, she was surprised and relieved to see a score of 99.

Finally! I've been wondering why I feel so different from my sisters and my mom. Why do I hide in my room when they start arguing and get loud? Why do I leave the room when they watch movies with violence and blood? And that's why I can't handle spicy food! I thought I was just a really strange person. I'm not strange; I'm just different.

Let's explore how you feel about the quiz results. (You can download this section at http://www.newharbinger.com/54032.)

Which quiz questions did you relate to most strongly?

What emotions are you feeling about learning you are highly sensitive?

Thinking about your day so far, what are some thoughts and feelings you've had that you now realize relate to your high sensitivity? Circle the terms that apply to you.

Curiosity	Relief	Happiness
Skepticism	Overwhelm	Anxiety
Enthusiasm	Irritation	Delight
Peace	Confusion	Joy
Fear		

Which five of the items on the quiz seemed *most* like you?

ABOUT THE HSP BRAIN

Is being an HSP an actual thing? Yes! The term "highly sensitive person" was created by Dr. Aron, who did research after she noticed that some people truly seemed more sensitive than others.

Dr. Aron noticed these HSPs were sensitive to feelings, light, sound, touch, and taste, and to everything around them. She also noticed that they tended to be empathetic, creative, and deep thinking. Dr. Aron noticed this about herself, too, and began exploring this more after a therapist told her she seemed to be very sensitive, in general (Morissette 2017).

She thought there should be a name for people with this type of sensitivity (also known as sensory processing sensitivity) so that others could understand them more and so they could also understand themselves. Most of all, Dr. Aron wanted it to be known that HSPs experience life differently because their brains are, in fact, different!

These facts about the HSP brain all give your brain superpowers (Daniels 2021).

Fact: The HSP brain works harder than the brains of most other people.

There is more intense activation in the *cingulate* and *premotor* areas of the brain, the parts that manage visual and attention processing. That means your five senses take in information and your brain makes you experience your five senses very strongly.

Fact: The HSP brain has more mirror neurons.

Mirror neurons are brain neurons associated with human empathy. This means that you can pick up on what emotions other people are experiencing when others can't. You may know when people are angry or disappointed even if they don't say a word. Having many mirror neurons can also help you understand others' intentions and motives.

Fact: The HSP brain gives you strong, vivid emotions.

Your emotions are extra powerful because of the *ventromedial prefrontal cortex* (vmPFC), the part of your brain that tells you about the emotions you're feeling. This gives you the experience of your emotions being definite, authentic, and crystal clear as they come over you, and that can feel intense!

Fact: The HSP brain uses serotonin differently.

Neurotransmitters are chemical substances that carry messages from one nerve to the next. The neurotransmitter serotonin helps the neurons in your brain communicate with each other about your emotions and also helps stabilize those emotions. The HSP brain has a harder time holding on to serotonin, so you may have to make a greater effort to smooth out emotions that feel extra powerful. On the other hand, it gives you a unique talent for learning from experience and knowing what to do when you feel those strong emotions.

Fact: The HSP brain uses dopamine differently.

Dopamine is another neurotransmitter. It helps you boot up to feel interested in and excited about tasks you need to do. It alerts your nervous system to get going and make things happen so you can feel great about what is happening. But since the HSP nervous system is already more alert than the nervous systems in other people, you actually don't need as much dopamine to feel motivated. And that's why hectic, busy, in-your-face environments can feel like too much!

Fact: The HSP brain uses norepinephrine differently.

The neurotransmitter norepinephrine helps you manage stress and keeps your emotions from adding to stress. It also makes vivid emotions even more vivid. This would explain why your friends may be able to watch tragic news stories on social media, but you may not feel you can take doing that.

Fact: The insula in the HSP brain is more intensely activated among HSPs than non-HSPs.

The *insula* (or, more formally, *insular cortex*) is the region of the brain involved with consciousness and emotion. Your brain's insula helps you understand what you are feeling in your body; for example, pain, hunger, and emotions. This is why HSPs may be hyperaware of all kinds of sensations.

Fact: The HSP brain's middle temporal gyrus (MTG) is especially active.

The *middle temporal gyrus* is the region of the brain involved with audiovisual emotional recognition and other processes. Your brain's MTG helps you interpret what your five senses are taking in and what you feel about that. It helps you know what you think and feel about loud sounds, bright lights, strong smells, and other people's emotional reactions.

Here's an example of how and why it helps to know that your brain works in a unique way. Because your brain processes information in such a different way, you may often make decisions differently than others do. As you take in data through your five senses and feel emotions responding to the data, you may notice that the decision-making process is gradual and careful instead of instant or impulsive. This may be why you would dislike being pressured or rushed when you have to decide about something major in your life or even something that seems minor to others. The more you know about your brain, the more comfortable and confident you'll feel.

What fact or facts about the HSP brain made you think *Yes, that's me!* when you read about them?

What three facts about the HSP brain interested you most and made you want to learn more?

Jack, age fifteen, said he was never interested in details of how his brain works until he found out he was an HSP.

I'm not really into science—I'm more into history and music. I zoned out during biology and did the same thing in chemistry. When I read about my brain being different, I got interested. I've known since I was little that I have trouble with noise and bright lights. When I study, I need the light to be super dim, or else I can't think straight. When my dad tries to tell me bright light is better for studying, I tell him about my MTG, and he can't argue with that!

Being highly sensitive may sometimes make you feel that you are on a different wavelength from others around you—and very often you are. Your emotions and five senses respond strongly to your environment, noticing things that other people don't. The same differences in your brain that make you highly sensitive also make you observant, perceptive, intuitive, compassionate, thoughtful, considerate, and self-aware.

As an HSP, your brain is enhanced so you can move through life in a way to notice more around you and respond more strongly to what you notice. Research on the way HSP brains work shows that some of your HSP traits are probably genetic, and some of your HSP traits formed gradually when you were very young—when you were a baby or even before you were born.

That means the way you are is not a problem—it is a gift. Research also estimates that up to 30 percent of people can be classified as HSPs, so you are definitely not alone!

And despite what you may have heard some people say, you are *not* just shy, picky, selfish, or weird. Some of those labels are downright offensive to HSPs, and even seemingly neutral words like "shy" or "picky" can make an HSP feel criticized or misunderstood. Being repeatedly labeled like this might make you feel as if you don't fit in.

Fifteen-year-old Stella says she has felt that way a lot:

> I go to a huge high school, and it seems like there are crowds everywhere. The noise in the hall and in the cafeteria bothers me a lot. I can't get much space, even in the bathroom, because there are a jillion girls in there gossiping. My friends call me a hermit, but I'm really not. They don't understand that I can be a great friend and I can be as much fun to hang out with as anyone else. I just need some space, and six hours is a long time to be in a building with two thousand other people.

Stella felt "hermit" was inaccurate for her. How about for you? Here are some possible ways to describe an HSP. Which words do you relate to most? You can download this list at http://www.newharbinger.com/54032. Circle the words you relate to most.

Perceptive	Observant	Careful
Empathetic	Compassionate	Gentle
Thoughtful	Deep	Considerate
Tuned-in	Understanding	Patient
Intuitive	Complex	Tactful
Private	Peaceful	

INTROVERT OR EXTROVERT?

Since HSPs often need alone time and tend to avoid crowds and noise, it may be incorrectly assumed that they are always introverts. *Introversion* is about an inward focus and using that inward focus as an energy source. Focusing on the outer world of people and social interactions drains an introvert's energy. *Extroversion* is about an outward focus and using that outward focus as an energy source. Extroverts feel more and more energetic as they interact with others and pay attention to the outer world.

An HSP extrovert may sometimes need to step away from sensory or emotional overwhelm, but they may be ready sooner to step back into the environment and more interested in doing so than their introverted HSP counterparts would be.

It may surprise you to know that around 30 percent of HSPs tend more toward extroversion, having an outward focus but with highly sensitive traits (Aron 2023). What this means is that high sensitivity is not necessarily introversion and not necessarily shyness—it is about how sensations and emotions are processed. You can be an HSP whether you're more inward focused or more outward focused!

TYPES OF HIGH SENSITIVITY

In daily life, being highly sensitive can look different for different people. In fact, there are seven types of sensitivity an HSP may have.

High Sensitivity to Emotions

You may have noticed that you have strong emotions and that you seem to feel them more deeply than some of your friends do. This is because of your extrasensitive nervous system, which allows your emotions to be intense and long-lasting. You may spend a lot of time feeling your emotions and may also need a lot of time to fully feel and understand them. This could be true whether you're feeling anger, joy, grief, or disappointment.

In addition, HSPs are often very tuned into the emotional atmosphere of a room. You may feel upset when others are upset in your class or in your home. It may upset you to hear about tragic events that have happened to other people. This ability to feel emotions deeply and strongly can make you highly empathetic, feeling others' emotions as if they were yours. This can be a superpower, but it can also be exhausting!

What are the emotions you tend to feel most strongly?

Russell, age sixteen, said he almost called his parents to come pick him up from band camp because he was upset and could not get enough time in a private place to work through his emotions.

So we were at band camp, and my best friend found out he didn't get picked as trumpet section leader. He should have gotten it—he was by far the best player and was also a better leader than the person the band director picked. He was devastated, and so was I. I know it happened to him and not to me, but I felt it pretty much the same way he did. It wasn't fair, and now he was going to have to take orders from somebody who didn't have his talent and didn't deserve to be the leader. It made me angry. It made me sad. It just felt overwhelming. I tried to find a place away from the practice field to sort it out and just feel all the bad stuff, but everyone kept coming up to me and asking me what was wrong. I felt that the world was an unfair place.

TIPS

Know that your emotions are never wrong—you feel what you feel, and that is totally okay!

Whenever possible, allow yourself alone time to fully experience and sort through your emotions.

High Sensitivity to Pain

Physical pain is something most people dread, but HSPs may experience it even more intensely than others do. This is because your nervous system is also highly sensitive.

Research has shown that HSPs probably have a lower pain threshold and lower pain tolerance than others do, so you may be experiencing physical pain in a way that feels like it hurts more than your parents or doctors expect.

You might also be more aware than the average person is of small changes in the way you're feeling physically—there actually is more going on in your body. This does not mean that you're weak or that you're a crybaby; you truly are experiencing more pain and sharper pain than others do. This could be true when you have headaches, stomachaches, a twisted ankle, or a bee sting.

Can you think of a time when you were hurting physically but it was hard to convince others that you were in a lot of pain?

TIP

Don't keep your pain to yourself just because others may say you're overreacting. You are the expert on your body and on how you're feeling, so feel free to speak up when you're hurting.

High Sensitivity to Sound

Being highly sensitive to sound means you might be more strongly impacted by noise and even to music than others. You may be bothered by loud noises and sudden sounds, and this could make you feel overwhelmed and upset. You might strongly dislike music that doesn't make you feel good. You might intensely love music that does make you feel good.

Take some time to reflect on these questions:

Does this sound like you? Are you highly sensitive to sound?

What are some sounds that you've noticed and were sensitive to?

What are some pleasant sounds that you actually like? What do you like about them?

What is a special song or piece of music that makes you feel good? Go listen to that song. When it is over, take a minute to reflect on how it makes you feel.

If you are highly sensitive to sound, you might also notice sounds that others aren't aware of, like humming noises in the background, conversations on the other side of the room, the sound of a clock ticking, or music coming from down the street.

TIPS

If you find yourself in a loud environment, try stepping away to find a private room or quiet corner. You can also try wearing earplugs or noise-canceling headphones.

It's okay to let friends and family members know when you've started to feel overwhelmed or bothered by noise.

High Sensitivity to Touch

Certain sensations from touching textures could be overwhelming and even stressful for you if they feel too scratchy and rough. This could happen with tags in clothing or with bedsheets and blankets. Clothes could make you feel uncomfortable if they are too tight, such as restrictive waistbands on pants or a skirt or jeans that fit like a second skin.

You might feel overstimulated by crowds, not just because of the noise but also because of people touching you and bumping into you. It might feel uncomfortable to be touched repeatedly or even to be hugged.

Temperatures could also affect you more than they affect others, both inside and outside. You may have extra discomfort when you feel cold.

What is the most comfortable environment in a room you can imagine? Describe the comfiest chair or sofa and the perfect temperature.

TIPS

To manage your sensitivity to touch, you may need to take extra steps to create a comfortable and soothing environment, such as wearing soft, comfortable clothing; using soft bedding; or avoiding rough or scratchy fabrics.

It's also important to communicate your needs to others and advocate for yourself when you are feeling uncomfortable or overstimulated by touch.

To try to be as comfortable as possible, you might want to pay close attention to what you wear, choosing soft clothing, sleeping on soft bedding, and knowing how to change the temperature on the thermostat in the room. It's okay to tell friends and family members that the way fabric, surfaces, and air temperatures feel matters to you and affects you. It's not being too picky or being difficult. There's nothing wrong with wanting to feel comfortable.

High Sensitivity to Sight

Being highly sensitive to what you see means that you could be strongly affected by visuals: colors, brightness, patterns, and the way visuals change and move.

You probably notice subtle details that others might not see, like shadows changing and moving and how glaringly bright or softly dim lighting is in a room. This sensitivity to visuals could mean you get overstimulated by looking at things that are bold or bright, but you may also have a good eye for the beauty of nature and art.

What are some of your favorite colors and color combinations? What are some of the most beautiful sights in each season of the year?

TIPS

You may want to keep your stress level low by using soft lighting in your bedroom and other rooms in your home.

Avoid having a lot of clutter in the places you sleep or study.

Whenever you can, spend time surrounded by nature and what you find to be beautiful and soothing.

Let friends and family know what you like and what stresses you out.

High Sensitivity to Taste

Being highly sensitive to taste means that you might have intense reactions—positive and negative—to food and drink. You might find certain seasonings and spices too overwhelming. You might also dislike some textures of food and reject them because of how they feel on your tongue.

It could be that you notice differences between the same food made with varying recipes. You could find one version of a salad dressing just fine and another version of the same dressing too intense or lumpy.

Looking at the positive, this could make you kind of an expert about differences in food preparation, and friends may rely on you to tell them whether they've done a good job cooking or whether a restaurant has good food or not. On the other hand, you might even have a bad digestive reaction to foods that overwhelm you with their flavor.

What are some foods and flavorings that affect you this way?

TIPS

You should avoid foods that you know you don't react well to.

There are ways to let friends and family know you're sensitive to taste in a way that does not criticize their cooking or their food choices. You can tell them you're sure the food is really tasty—it's just that you are wired with a super sensitive ability to taste, and so even food that is seasoned and flavored normally could taste extra strong to you.

High Sensitivity to Smell

Being highly sensitive to smell means that you may be aware of scents—even slight and subtle scents—in your environment more so than others are. You might find certain smells overpowering and need to leave the room. Fumes from cleaning products, strong perfume, air freshener scents, cooking smells, and cigarette smoke are all examples of smells that may be overpowering.

Because of your sensitivity to smell, overpowering scents could cause more than just stress—they could cause headaches and nausea. On the positive side, you might have a special love for delicate, soothing smells from candles, flowers, and light perfumes.

What are three scents that have overwhelmed you in the past? What are three of your favorite scents?

TIPS

Try to avoid spending time in places with overpowering smells, like crowded restaurants and perfume counters in stores.

It is okay to tell the people you're hanging out with that you are sensitive to smell and need to step away for a few minutes.

WHAT'S NEXT?

Now that you've learned the basics about being an HSP, let's talk about how you can present this information to family, teachers, and friends. In the next three chapters we'll explore ways of approaching these conversations.

CHAPTER 2

HELPING YOUR FAMILY UNDERSTAND

Now that you know you really do have more intense and deeper sensitivities than most other people, how do you talk about it with your parents and siblings?

It might feel challenging to start a discussion, and for good reason. First, you are still exploring what being highly sensitive means to *you*, so it can be hard to talk to someone else about what you're still trying to figure out. Second, you are trying to describe to someone else how you experience your life, and it can be difficult to find the words to match the feelings.

TALKING WITH YOUR PARENTS

Sixteen-year-old Annisa said she waited two weeks after discovering her own highly sensitive nature before talking to her father about it.

> I had a lot to think about after the therapy session where my therapist and I first talked about what an HSP is. I guess I tend to be pretty private about my feelings, so I needed that time to process the whole thing. After a couple of weeks of journaling and reading up on HSP, I was ready to bring it up with my dad, but I'm glad I waited until then. This was something I needed to have as just mine for a while.

And it really is *yours* to do with as you wish! That includes the choice of who to talk to first. In some cases, that person might not be a family member but a teacher (see chapter 3) or your best friend (see chapter 4). For now, let's explore what it might be like to tell your parents about your new understanding of how you're wired.

Factors to Consider

Your mood: If you're feeling down, it might be better to save the conversation for another time. It's hard to seem focused or enthusiastic when you are having a lot of negative thoughts and emotions.

Your energy level: If you're feeling drained of energy at the moment, you might run out of steam before fully explaining what it means to be highly sensitive. Wait until you have the mental and emotional stamina to start the conversation, give examples, and answer your parents' questions.

Your parent's mood: If the parent you are aiming to talk to seems grouchy, stressed, hangry, or tired, you should wait until they are none of those things. If you're not sure, you can ask whether it's a good time to talk.

The setting: As a highly sensitive person, you probably already know how much setting matters when it comes to feeling comfortable. When you're considering bringing up the subject of who you are and what you need, also consider whether the back porch on a Sunday afternoon would be better than the car during rush-hour traffic. Consider where you feel most relaxed and at peace in addition to where your parents feel relaxed and at peace.

When you think the time and place are right, give it a try. It might end up being several small conversations rather than one big one.

Annisa approached her father while they were out walking the dog on a Saturday morning.

I talked to my dad about my sensitivity, and he was supportive. I could actually tell he was interested in it himself, which made sense since we're a lot alike. He said he never knew there was a name for being sensitive about everything. When I talked to my mom, it was different. She didn't react well at first, because she thought it sounded like I was trying to make excuses for my picky eating and for liking to be alone in my room so much. She said she was worried about me. It was hard to keep going with the conversation, but I stuck with it, and she said she might be willing to read up on HSP stuff.

Annisa said the talk with her mother was a good start that led to better communication between them, though it took some time.

Questions You May Have

What if I talk to my parents several times and they still don't get it?

If that happens, don't give up hope that they might be more open to it later. There was a time when *you* didn't yet know about HSPs and all the ways sensitivity affects your life, but the time came when that changed, and you started to learn about it. In the same way, if you have one or both parents who either don't understand (or don't seem to want to understand), things may be different down the road, as in the case of Annisa's mother.

Should I talk about the brain science aspect?

There are two circumstances when it could be helpful to talk about that with your parents. One is when you have a parent who is very science oriented and very fact oriented and might not be as open to hearing about your emotions or sensory experiences. That parent may be interested in mirror neurons and dopamine, and a discussion about those could be a gateway to more personal discussions later.

The other circumstance when it could be helpful to bring up the science is when you yourself are strongly interested in it. Your interest may be contagious, and your parent(s) would be able to see how important the subject is to you.

How can I start a conversation?

Here are some of the many different ways to open the conversation:

I just took an interesting quiz about being a highly sensitive person…

You know how you're always telling me I'm "too sensitive"?

Remember that time I wore earplugs to the football game?

I just learned the coolest thing about myself!

You know how I hate to wear scratchy clothes?

I can't sit through a horror movie. Now I know why!

So, I was in the bookstore and found this book about highly sensitive teens…

Did you know there's such a thing as a highly sensitive person?

Does it have to be an in-person conversation? Can I do it by text or email?

It doesn't *have* to be any certain way. If it's more comfortable for you to express yourself in writing, write a draft and see how it feels. You can finalize the draft and send it to your parents, or keep it as a draft and continue to think about it. The process of writing down what you'd like to say could help you sort through the many thoughts and feelings you may be having.

TALKING WITH YOUR SIBLINGS

Explaining your sensitivity and process of self-discovery to your siblings is not totally different from trying to talk to your parents about it. The right time, place, and mood are still important factors. But there are some things to consider with brothers and sisters that don't apply as much to parents.

Factors to Consider

Age (yours and theirs): Your parents are a generation or two ahead of you and have been responsible for your well-being all your life. To some degree, they have always served as guides. Your siblings may be close to you in age, or they may be nearly a generation older or younger than you are. They may be young adults or still in diapers. How you would talk to them (or whether they are even old enough to understand what you mean) depends on their age.

Siblings who are already young adults (college age or older) might be familiar with the idea of the HSP or at least have done some self-discovery work of their own. Or they might not be interested in psychology or temperament, but they may have enough maturity to listen to you with an open mind.

Siblings who are around your age might be interested and tell you so or might be uninterested and tell you so, depending on their personality or on the type of relationship you have. Their reaction might also depend on whether they are annoyed with you at the moment.

Younger siblings might not be mature enough yet to even understand what the word "sensitivity" means, but if your sibling is nine rather than five, it could be worth trying to talk about it with them, especially if this sibling shows signs of possibly being an HSP like you.

Personality: No matter how old your sibling is, consider their personality before launching into the conversation. Is your sibling someone who doesn't talk about feelings much? Don't be surprised if their reaction is quiet and seems unenthusiastic. Is your sibling someone who teases people and makes serious topics into jokes? It's likely you'll get a teasing, joking response. Just like you want your siblings to let you be you, try to let them be themselves in the way they respond to you, even if it's disappointing to you.

Relationship: Consider the unique relationship you have with each sibling. With one, you might have a friendly rivalry, so it might make sense that they don't want to let you go on thinking you're special. With another, you might have a lot of conflict and petty arguments, and you might not want to share your deep thoughts and feelings with them. The sibling who has always understood you might understand you very well when you talk about your high level of sensitivity. An important word in all this is "might." You can't be sure how siblings will respond when you talk about this, so be prepared for surprises and possible disappointments.

Max, age eighteen, was surprised he had trouble talking to his twin brother about high sensitivity.

We're fraternal twins, so I didn't expect him to have thoughts identical to mine, but I was upset when he didn't care about it at all. I mean, he didn't even pretend to be interested. I kept talking about how sad and angry I get watching the world news, and he just kept staring at his phone, scrolling. I got mad and said that was the last time I would ever mention it to him.

Max had thought his brother would understand. They were the same age, played the same sports, and were headed to the same college, yet he walked away from the attempted conversation deeply disappointed.

A full year later, Max reported that his brother, still uninterested in talking about Max's high sensitivity, sent him a link to an article about HSPs and music preferences. There was no comment attached—only the link.

Just like with parents, siblings may not seem interested or accepting at first but could become more open to the idea later. Don't try to force them to be supportive. Think about the way you may not like harsh environments like glaring lights and angry voices. If you try to make them agree with you or try to get your parents to back you against a sibling who is not an HSP, you would be, in a way, like a too-bright light or a loud argument.

TALKING WITH YOUR GRANDPARENTS

Should you talk to your grandparents about being an HSP? If you would like to share this part of yourself with them, it could be a great conversation that strengthens your bond with them. But, as with the cautions about setting, mood, personality, and relationship when it comes to talking to parents and siblings, the same factors may apply with grandparents.

You have a unique relationship with each grandparent, so adjust your way of talking about it to match the relationship. Being several generations younger than your grandparents could mean you have to explain it from a different angle, but on the other hand, you might find that your seventy-five-year-old grandmother understands what you mean because of her many life experiences and her interest in you.

The main thing is to share something you've learned about yourself without expectation of a specific response from them.

TALKING WITH STEPPARENTS AND STEPSIBLINGS

If you're part of a blended family, you likely already know that family relationships are not cookie-cutter and that the blending process happens over time, sometimes with ease and sometimes with difficulty. Stepparents and stepsiblings have likely noticed that you are sensitive, so it could improve overall family communication to tell them more about your preferences and needs.

You may feel every bit as close to your stepparent as you do to your birth parents and may be eager to share what you've learned about yourself with them. On the other hand, you may have a stepparent that you don't feel as close to.

The same is true with your stepsiblings. Just as with any sibling, consider their age, personality, and the kind of relationship you have with them. Consider what kinds of things they usually share about themselves with *you*.

It's always your call what to share about yourself and how much detail to go into.

Q & A

What if my whole family is highly sensitive? Does that mean they'll understand what an HSP is?

Maybe, but maybe not. Family members could tend to be sensitive without being *as* sensitive across the board as you are. They may not relate to every element of sensitivity the way you do. It's also possible that because they tend to be sensitive, they may react negatively to the term "highly sensitive person" and feel as if you're trying to label them.

If your parents and siblings are generally in sync with you about the environment you prefer, that's a good thing. Grant them the freedom to be who they are, and they will be more likely to do the same for you!

What if nobody in the family is anything like me and none of them understand what I'm talking about?

If that's the case, you've probably already dealt with some frustration over feeling different or at times misunderstood. That can be upsetting, especially if you feel like your emotions are not understood.

But there are other ways of looking at your situation. As tough as it can be to feel like the rest of the family is out of step with you, there are probably some ways that you *are* in step with them. Maybe you and your family all love to go hiking and have fun doing it together. Maybe you have in common with them that you love cats and enjoy the family pets.

It's even possible that other family members—maybe your dad or your brother—have some way that *they* feel out of step with everyone else. Maybe they feel their sense of humor is different or their favorite foods are different.

You can try to think about differences as being normal and expected while at the same time working on helping family members understand you better.

Should I show family members my High Sensitivity Indicator Quiz result?

Yes, if you think it would help them to understand what an HSP is and how you fit in that category. Some people enjoy taking tests and quizzes, and some people roll their eyes at them. Anytime you want to show people something that's important to you, be prepared that they may not react like you hoped they would. Show them the HSI and your results if you want to; just don't let yourself expect a specific response from them.

WHEN TO TALK WITH YOUR FAMILY

Does all this talk about family members, explanation, risk, uncertainty, and patience feel draining to you? HSPs tend to feel emotionally and physically exhausted from intense conversations. And there's also the possible exhaustion from all the noise inside your head as you try to plan how to start the discussions.

Just know that there is no rush to talk to anyone about your thoughts and experiences. Wait until you feel comfortable and ready to give these conversations a try. No pressure.

CHAPTER 3

COPING AT SCHOOL

Did you know you spend almost as many hours at school as you do at home (not counting the hours that you're asleep)?

School can provide lots of challenges for a highly sensitive person. From fluorescent lights to the roar of crowds in the cafeteria to high-conflict drama in the locker room, the environment can be uncomfortable.

Because of that, it's important that your teachers know about high sensitivity and how it affects the way you learn. But with all the papers teachers have to grade, and all the students teachers are responsible for instructing, how can you get them to understand?

One way is for your parents to talk to them about it. If you think your parents understand enough about high sensitivity and how it affects you at school, it may work well for them to have a conference with your teachers to explain it. Your parents could take the lead in letting teachers know things like how you react to noisy talking in class; how you feel when class discussions or assignments cover topics of violence or tragedy; and how room lighting affects your performance on tests.

If you don't want your parents to intervene for you (or if they don't want to), there are other options.

Another way is for you to talk to the school counselor and let the counselor discuss it with your teachers. School counselors are specially trained to communicate with teachers when students need support or understanding. You could talk to the counselor about discovering that you're an HSP and speak in detail about what you like about school and what you dislike. Because school counselors are experts at listening carefully to students and helping with problem solving, they may be able to be the link between you and your teachers.

A third way is for you to talk with your teachers directly. This would be a good option if you don't want a third party—your parents or a school counselor—talking about you to the teachers. This would also be a good way to go if you feel confident that you understand what you need and know how to explain it.

Carmen, age fourteen, wrote her social studies teacher a long email about her high sensitivity, reminding him about a recent time she was upset during class.

> Remember when we had the presentations last month about South American countries and mine was about Venezuela? And those guys in the back of the room were making fun of the names of the cities? You probably didn't understand why I started crying and why I pretended to have a headache so you would let me leave class. Both of my parents were born in Venezuela, and I feel like it's my home country, even though I've never been there. It felt like they were making fun of me when they were mocking the cities. It really hurt my feelings. I hope you won't say what everybody else does when I tell them things like this. 'You're too sensitive' is all I hear, over and over again.

After her teacher read the email, he invited her to meet with him before school. They talked about the incident when the kids had laughed at her presentation, and he said he now had a better understanding of why she was upset and why she asked to leave class that day. He listened as Carmen explained what an HSP is and about the HSP characteristics she has. The talk with the social studies teacher went so well that Carmen eventually talked with her other teachers and felt that they were all supportive.

WHEN TEACHERS AREN'T SO AGREEABLE

Carmen had a good experience approaching her teachers and opening up to them. But as you may know, teachers vary in personality and teaching style, and some of them may not see sensitivity as something they should consider.

High sensitivity is something you can try to explain to them, but it isn't something they can measure or see physical proof of, like a fever or 20/20 vision. And because being an HSP is not yet recognized as a medically or psychologically diagnosable condition, it isn't something you can prove or force teachers to accept.

With teachers who think the high sensitivity is a problem that needs to be "cured" by you toughening up or maturing, you may need to try any or all of the following strategies:

Getting the support of your parents

In chapter 2, we talked about the possible range of reactions from your parents, from immediate support and understanding to skepticism and rejection. When a teacher resists your requests for help, the best solution is to have your parents take the lead in the back-and-forth discussions that might be necessary.

Getting the support of the school counselor

School counselors can be your go-to resource for any difficulty you're having at school. They can be very helpful acting as an advocate for you if you're hitting a brick wall trying to communicate with teachers. It may even be that your school counselors already know about HSPs and have studied it as part of their training. If they haven't heard of it, odds are good that they will be interested in learning about it.

Getting the support of your pediatrician

A doctor's opinion usually gets the attention of school staff, from teachers to counselors to principals. Even though being an HSP is not a medical diagnosis, a letter from your doctor stating that you tend to be highly sensitive in the ways that you truly are (for example, sensitive to disturbing content in lessons, sensitive to loud noises), and that this sensitivity could lead to anxiety or to physical symptoms, could influence school staff to listen to your concerns.

Getting the support of your therapist

A letter from your therapist would work similarly to the way a letter from your pediatrician would work, with school staff probably being more open to hearing you out if a licensed mental health therapist who knows you well states that your sensitivity is real and is in no way an excuse you're trying to make.

Gathering links to websites and videos about HSP

Although teachers are very busy with stacks of papers to grade and lesson plans to write, they may be willing to read or watch short articles and videos about HSPs and their needs. Some teachers may immediately agree to take a look, and some teachers may agree to it but not actually do it. This is another situation when you shouldn't try to force them to give your high sensitivity the respect you'd like them to. Provide them with the information and give them space to read it or view it when they can.

How School Staff Members Can and Can't Help

What they can do

The most important thing school staff members can do for you is to listen to you with an open mind, even if what you're describing is very different from their own life experiences. Feeling listened to goes a long way when you're upset or uncomfortable.

Another thing they can do is give you a safe haven: a place in the school building you can go to when your senses or emotions get overwhelmed. This could be a school counselor's office, the media center, or any other quiet place with school staff in the room or nearby. You may be able to make a formal or informal agreement with the school administration or with individual teachers that allows you to exit the classroom, gym, or cafeteria if you need a short time away to calm down or just to sort through your thoughts and feelings.

Teachers can collaborate with you on a subtle signal to let them know you're struggling. For example, you can use a certain code word or hand gesture to let them know without the other students noticing that you need to leave the room or are starting to feel physical discomfort.

They can let you email them to share more detail about what is going on with you on days you're not feeling your best. That way, they can pay closer attention to what you're saying than they could if you try to talk to them right before or after class. Plus, it's more private.

They can help you handle constructive criticism when they give you feedback on your schoolwork but make an effort not to criticize you in harsher-than-necessary ways. Some teachers will not be willing to do this and will be harsh or even unkind in the feedback they give, but that doesn't mean they don't care or that they dislike you. Some teachers believe the best way to help students develop intellectually is to be tough and stern; other teachers may be more sensitive to *your* sensitivity, giving you honest feedback but doing it in a friendlier way.

What they can't do

Teachers will not be able to be flexible for you to the point that other students feel you're getting special treatment on a regular basis. This can be a judgment call for the teacher to make when it comes to how many times they would let you put your head down on your desk when noise or bright lights bother you. It can be a judgment call when it comes to how big a deal it is for you to be able to leave the classroom multiple times in a month.

It could make it hard for the teacher to maintain order in the classroom if the other students think you're getting to do whatever you want to. If the teacher seems to be favoring you over others, parents might hear about it and then complain.

This means that it is perfectly fine for you to ask for support and flexibility from teachers and school staff—just be aware that they may not be able to grant you all of it.

WHAT ABOUT 504 PLANS?

Can you get a 504 Plan for being an HSP? The short answer is maybe.

In the United States, all K–12 schools are required to offer 504 Plans to students who need adjustments to their learning environment. The term "504 Plan" comes from Section 504 of a civil rights law passed in 1973. This section gives students with differences and disabilities equal access to all aspects of school. The idea is that if there are any barriers to you being able to learn, a 504 Plan helps remove them.

504 Plans don't change what a student is being taught or what the academic standards are—they simply allow flexibility in *how* a student learns. For example, a student who has color blindness might be given handouts that show information classified some other way than by color. Students with hypoglycemia (low blood sugar) might be allowed to keep certain types of candy in their pockets or purses to prevent them from fainting at school.

504 Plans are created based on diagnosed medical or psychological problems, and since HSP is not yet in that category, it can't be the reason for getting a 504 Plan. But if you have conditions that are *connected* to your high sensitivity, like generalized anxiety disorder, migraine headaches, depression, or gastrointestinal problems, you may be able to get one.

Here's how it works: A parent emails the school's 504 Plan coordinator and asks for an evaluation. The coordinator schedules a meeting with you, your parents, some of your teachers, and other school staff. The school staff members on this committee will then consider data from your doctors and/or your therapist along with data from all your teachers before deciding whether you need a 504 Plan.

A typical 504 Plan for a high school student who has an anxiety disorder might include the "safe haven" idea along with prompts from the teacher allowing the student time to prepare before being called on in class.

504 Plans are confidential, so teachers and school staff don't talk about them in front of other students.

Remember that if you don't qualify for a 504 Plan, you might still be able to make some informal agreements with your teachers.

DEALING WITH CONFLICT AT SCHOOL

Whether a school is small, middle-sized, or large, many students will have conflict with each other and with their teachers. Conflict is a normal part of life, but it can be upsetting to an HSP because of the impact on the emotions and the general harshness in voice and body language when people argue or are driven by anger.

How can an HSP cope five days a week observing (or experiencing) friend group drama, criticism from teachers, high-conflict rivalries, mean-spirited teasing, and bullying? One way is to talk to someone who cares and can help you problem solve.

Thirteen-year-old Micah refused to get out of the car one morning when his mother tried to drop him off at school. His mother said she was puzzled, since he had seemed fine when they left the house.

I honestly didn't know what to do. Micah just sat there like a statue and shook his head every time I asked him to get out of the car. He wouldn't tell me what was wrong. I knew he had been upset a few times about getting teased in homeroom, but he just got so extreme about it, out of nowhere.

But for Micah, it wasn't out of nowhere. He said it had been building up for weeks, and as he thought about the homeroom situation that morning in the carpool line, he decided to take a stand.

Mom says it confused her, but I had been mad for a long time about the stuff going on. It wasn't just that people were teasing me. It was that they were picking on the girl who sits behind me, too. They were calling her names and making fun of the way she talks. Messing with me was one thing but messing with that girl and making her cry—that was just too much. It made me feel like I was being slimed every time I walk through the door, and it ruined the rest of the day. I just felt like I couldn't go back. Something inside me said no.

Micah's mother called the seventh-grade school counselor to tell her he was refusing to go back to school, and that call led to a meeting with the counselor and the homeroom teacher to listen to Micah's concerns. Once the teacher realized what had been going on in the classroom, she changed the seating chart and addressed the teasing. Micah agreed to go back to school and said he now understands he can go see the counselor anytime he feels "slimed."

For some HSPs, classmates' behavior may be what bothers them the most. For other HSPs, the struggle may be more with the general rowdy, loud environment in the hallways or on the bus. And for others, the issue may be the flickering fluorescent lights and uncomfortable desks. What these have in common is a roughness or harshness that's unpleasant for a person who wants more of a "smooth ride" at school.

STEP AWAY OR SPEAK UP

Sometimes you can step away from harshness and roughness in the environment by changing to a different seat in the classroom (with the teacher's permission). You can step away by having the safe-haven agreement we talked about earlier. You can step away by leaving a group chat that feels toxic to you. And you can even step away by wearing noise-canceling headphones when and where they are allowed at school.

When you can't step away, speak up. You can do that by sharing concerns with your parents, the school counselor, a teacher, or a close friend. You can do it by telling friends when you don't want to hear any more gossip. You can let your friends know what you *do* want to talk about, where you *do* want to sit, and what music you *do* want to hear. When any situation at school disturbs your peace, it is just as important to speak up about what would help you as it is to point out the problems.

Speaking up can be hard. In chapters 4 and 5, we'll explore how to help your friends understand your highly sensitive nature and how to be assertive in a way that fits your individual temperament. We'll talk more about stepping away from drama and conflict when you can and handling it skillfully when you can't.

CHAPTER 4

HELPING YOUR FRIENDS UNDERSTAND

We've talked about some possible ways to start conversations with your family members, but what about conversations with your friends?

Just as you've known for a while that there's something different about you compared to other people, your friends may have noticed this, too. Your friends may like you for who you are and may even have given you compliments about your sensitivity. But you may also have a few friends who ask you the same questions over and over again or try to persuade you to do things their way.

Take a moment to think about these friendships. Are there people you want to have in your life but who just don't seem to get it? Maybe they sincerely want to understand but don't have enough information. You can't control how other people interact with you, but you *can* let your friends know what being an HSP means and how it affects your life. Consider letting them in on everything you've learned.

Ava, age fifteen, said she told her friends in the drama club at school about being an HSP, with mixed results.

We were on the bus coming back from a one-act play competition, and I decided to tell some of my friends why I don't like to share a bus seat. One of them had rolled her eyes at me when I asked to sit alone on the bus trip. She called me a princess, like she was kidding. But to me, it was serious. So I talked to her and the other friends sitting in the seats around me. I explained that I'm not trying to be a princess—I'm just super sensitive in a whole bunch of ways. I explained that sometimes a noisy bus feels like too much. The friend who called me princess just kind of laughed it off. She didn't get it. But a few of the others did. And that was okay.

Ava was learning that she could decide how much to explain to her friends and that she could give some the short version and give others the long version.

DECIDING HOW MUCH TO SHARE

Your sensitivity is unique to you, and it is yours to talk about or not talk about. But how do you make that call? Here are some questions to ask yourself when you are considering opening up to a friend.

- Did this friend seem to understand me in the past when I talked about personal or complex issues?

- Have I been able to trust this friend with my thoughts and feelings in the past?

- Has this friend ever been open with me about their thoughts, feelings, and experiences?

- Do I know what outcome I am hoping for from the conversation?

- Can I handle the negative feelings I may experience if I try having this conversation and it does not go the way I'd hoped?

If you answered yes to most of these questions, this friend is probably one who makes you feel safe. If you answered no to most of these questions, ask yourself whether you truly feel comfortable opening up to this friend yet. If you haven't shared with many people, you might start with the friends you trust most and decide later about the others.

WAYS TO START

Once you've decided that there is someone you want to confide in, it can still be hard to start the conversation with them. How you begin a conversation depends on several Ws: who, what, where, when, and why. Use the following steps to make a plan for the conversation:

Who?

First, who is the friend you have in mind? Return to the questions above. Is this someone you feel safe with, or do you expect this to be a particularly difficult conversation? Consider how close and comfortable you find the friendship to be. You may find the conversation to be the most challenging or may feel the most anxious about a friend who is not really in your inner circle. As you go through the rest of the steps, keep in mind how you feel around this person. Knowing that can help you in your decision making.

What?

What do you want to tell your friend about—the big picture of your high sensitivity or something specific like your discomfort with violent movies? Decide how much you want to tell your friend about yourself and what you've learned.

Where?

Think about where you and your friend are or will be when you get ready to have this conversation. If you're walking down the hall to class, the place might not be right—too crowded and too loud. If you're hanging out at your house, you might not have enough privacy to talk about it. Look for a place where it is easy to talk without interruption or too much noise.

You could have the conversation virtually using a video platform. You could also do it via text, though it might be hard to know how well you're being understood if your friend can't hear your voice or see your face.

When?

If it's just one aspect of your sensitivity, you could start a conversation when those circumstances come up. For example, if you want them to know how you feel about violent movies, you might wait until you're discussing going to the movies and say something like: "In case you were ever wondering, I sometimes leave the room when we're streaming a movie because the violence is just too much for me."

If it's the big picture of your high sensitivity, you might want to ask your friend if this is a good time to talk about something important to you. If it's not a good time, see if you can plan for one. It's best to choose a time when you won't have to worry about being late to class or work. You might start by saying you're a highly sensitive person (or an HSP), and that means that you tend to be more sensitive than most when it comes to what you hear, see, taste, touch, and feel emotionally. It can be helpful to be ready with specific examples.

Why?

Think about what the purpose of the conversation is. Is it for a specific purpose, such as explaining to your friend why you don't want to go camping? Or is it for a more general purpose, to let your friend know some of the struggles you've had that you've been keeping to yourself? It can help to be very clear about your purpose before you start the conversation.

REQUESTS VS. CRITICISM

When you talk to your friends about your needs and preferences, they may mistakenly think that you're criticizing them. When you're trying to open up to your friends and tell them about your personal experiences with sensitivity, the last thing you'd want is for them to get upset and stop listening. You're trying to improve their understanding of you, not make it worse!

But what if you want to ask your friends to do some things differently now that they know you're sensitive about certain things? For example, after explaining to a friend that you are uncomfortable watching movies that have a lot of violent scenes in them, you might want to ask that, when you hang out at their house to stream a movie, they choose one that is mostly nonviolent. Another example of this would be asking your friends if the study group could meet in a study room at the public library rather than at the neighborhood coffeehouse because you need a quieter, less bustling atmosphere in order to study.

One way to make it more likely your friends won't feel you're attacking them when you have conversations like this is to make sure it sounds like a request instead of a complaint. Making a complaint is *telling* your friends they are doing something wrong. Making a request is *asking* them for a favor, and that will probably hit them differently, especially when you follow the request with sincere appreciation.

It could be something like this:

When we study tonight, can we try it at the public library instead of the coffee house? I have a hard time focusing with all the noise in the coffee house.

Thanks so much! I really appreciate that.

PATIENCE WITH MISTAKES AND CREDIT FOR TRYING

The conversations could go well, but your friends might slip up later and forget your preferences. Let's say that after a talk with your two best friends, they agreed not to rush you when it's time to leave the school cafeteria. You explained that you have a hard time when people pressure you to hurry, especially when you're trying to finish a meal. At the time, they said they understood and would remember to give you a five-minute warning before they were ready to leave for class. But a week later, one of them suddenly raised his voice and said "Hurry up! C'mon!" You were startled and felt yelled at by him. You also felt embarrassed to have this happen in front of everyone at the table.

If your friends slip up, try to be patient with them as they try to remember your needs and preferences. They might forget what they agreed to, or maybe they didn't understand your request as well as you think they did. If you feel your wishes were disregarded or misunderstood, here are two things you can do:

- Try to give your friend(s) the benefit of the doubt and assume they had good intentions. It's true that good intentions aren't enough sometimes, but they are quite different from *bad* intentions.

- Consider a redo of the conversation. The "when" would be important in this because it would be best to wait until you are no longer actively upset about the incident. The riskiest time to try to settle an issue is when feelings are still stirred up. Once you have had some time to let the feelings smooth out and settle down, you could journal about the incident or spend some quiet time thinking it through. Afterward, you could plan a time to have another conversation.

CONFLICT WITH FRIENDS

Conflict with friends can be especially painful for HSPs. You probably prefer that all your relationships be peaceful and harmonious—particularly your relationships with your friends. When people in your friend group are mad at each other (or even worse, mad at *you*), it may be hard for you to feel calm and hard for you to feel good about life.

Levi, age sixteen, said he almost felt like changing schools when some of his friends got mad at each other and then got mad at him because he wouldn't choose a side in the feud.

It was the worst feeling. I couldn't win. Either way, people were mad at me. And I really didn't agree with either side. I thought the whole thing was unnecessary and just really immature. I hated the pressure my friends put on me to give an opinion about who was right. I actually didn't go to school the next two days because I honestly had a headache and nausea over it. What I finally did was write the whole group a letter and tell them I just declined to be part of something so divisive. My parents talked me out of changing schools, and it blew over like everything does. I think my friends learned that I don't like that kind of conflict.

HSPs often dislike being pressured to do anything and often equally dislike intense negative communication. But since conflict is a normal part of human behavior and a normal part of life, there is no way to get away from pressure and conflict other than to become a hermit. And becoming a hermit would rob you of full joy of living. Instead of retreating to live in a cave, you can learn how to deal with conflict in your relationships. Here are some ways to do that:

- Keep reminding yourself that conflict is a normal part of life, and it is not necessarily harmful. You may not believe it at first, but keep reminding yourself of it anyway.

- Know that your preference for peaceful, kind communication can often help others because it sets an example they can follow.

- Remember what Levi said about conflict blowing over like everything does. He's right—eventually, conflict dies down, and most arguments are forgotten. Sometimes conflict can lead to permanent splits in friend groups and ends to friendships, but the drama and the angry words do stop.

- If conflict leads to splits in a friend group or ends a friendship, you can get through it and move forward with your life, making other friends. Sometimes friendship breakups happen because certain people may be better off as acquaintances or just class-mates—it does not mean they have to become enemies.

- If you ever do find that you have enemies, you don't need to agonize over that. Continue spending time with the people you know are friends you can count on, and let the ex-friends go.

CHAPTER 5

STANDING UP FOR YOURSELF

Now that you have tools and methods to talk to family, teachers, and friends about your high sensitivity, how do you go about speaking up in public settings or to people you don't know well?

This can be difficult, but you can learn to do it in a way that fits your personality and feels comfortable to you. The key word here is *comfortable*.

When *you* are comfortable and others can tell that you're comfortable, they're likely to accept what you say about your needs and preferences. The big question—how can you get comfortable enough with yourself to confidently speak up? There are two things important for you to know as you begin to work on this:

- Most people struggle to feel comfortable with themselves at times. It's not only you who feels awkward and uncomfortable in certain situations—even the most self-assured, popular people you know have wondered what to do or say and fumbled through a situation. Everybody fumbles through life at some times and feels unsure about what to say or do.

- Getting more comfortable with talking about what you need and prefer is a process, not an instant change. The more you try, the better you'll get at it. Is that hard to believe? This process can be compared to learning how to skate. You've probably seen beginners out on the rink, stumbling, falling, and waving their hands around awkwardly. That can be how it feels to speak up sometimes. But check in with that same skater after a week or two, and their moves look steadier and a bit smoother. Check in again after another few weeks, and their moves are clearly smoother. And that's the way it can be as you keep making attempts to speak up.

As you start your "skating," you may wonder, is it okay to tell strangers—like servers in restaurants and supermarket cashiers—what you want and need? The answer is yes. It is *always* okay to be your authentic self and to experience the world in the way that comes naturally to you. And there's nothing wrong with making your needs known.

Speak up, since no two people are exactly alike, and everybody has preferences!

HOW TO SPEAK UP

Trista, age sixteen, said she made the decision to be more authentic one night over a bowl of noodles.

> We all went out for Thai food after band practice, and I really wanted to spend the time with my friends, but I have a hard time finding anything on a Thai menu that isn't too spicy for me. We were ordering our food one by one, and when it was my turn, I froze because I didn't want anyone to know I was struggling. But I just decided to say what I was actually thinking. I mumbled something like "I'll have the pad thai, but if you can, please tone down the spices." I didn't apologize for it. Nobody laughed at me, and when my food came, it was at a spice level I could handle. After that, it got easier to speak up about a lot of other things, too.

Trista realized that she started to feel more okay about herself when she stopped apologizing for making requests and stopped pretending to be perfectly fine when she really wasn't.

Speaking up can be scary, though. Sometimes it's hard to know how to even start the first sentence. Here are some possible ways to start, whether you're talking about spicy food, cold temperatures, loud music, or harsh language:

"I would rather…"

"I don't want to…"

"I want to…"

"What works better for me is…"

"Y'all have fun—I'm going to go…"

"I think I'll just…"

"I need to…"

"I'm asking you…"

"Do you mind if I…"

"I like to…"

Now let's plug these into common situations you might have to deal with.

Sound:

Do you mind if I turn the volume down slightly?

See you later—I'm going to leave the concert early.

Touch:

I need to move to a different chair.

I like to cut the tags out of my shirts.

I'm going to grab a different blanket from the linen closet.

Sight:

I want to dim the lights a little.

I would rather study in the blue room.

Taste:

I would like mine without onions and peppers.

I think I'll just have toast instead of yogurt.

I've decided to have lunch on my own.

Smell:

I would rather go fragrance-free tonight.

I need to step outside the store for a sec—the scented candles are giving me a headache.

Pain:

I need to take some ibuprofen before we go out.

I think I'll just stay in today—my stomach's upset.

I don't want to arm-wrestle anymore today.

Emotion:

I would rather watch something else.

I'm going to head home early and let you guys finish your argument.

What works better for me is constructive criticism.

I'm asking you not to raise your voice at me.

Notice that none of these sentence starters or examples leave the person you're talking to confused about what you prefer. None are disrespectful or rude things to say.

And notice that they *all* put the power in your hands to change something about the situation.

BEING EMPOWERED: BOUNDARY SETTING FOR HSPs

Speaking up is a part of being kind to yourself. And being kind to yourself is important because it gives you some control over what life is like for you. You can't control *everything* from day to day, but you can control how you treat yourself and what you're willing to do to create the kind of life you want.

You may have heard the word "boundaries" used as a way of letting people know what you are and are not willing to accept. This is similar to how a property owner decides whether to put fences along their property lines. If they don't put up any fences, neighbors and strangers may end up walking on their property because they can take a shortcut across the lawn. If they *do* put fences up, neighbors and strangers know exactly where to stop, and the fence is there every time they try to walk across the lawn.

How do you know when your "fences" are strong enough and clear enough for people to notice and step back from? You will feel uncomfortable, at the very least, and possibly quite upset when your lawn gets walked on. Let those negative feelings be helpful signals to you that you need to create boundaries.

Creating Boundaries

Fences speak for themselves unless they're invisible. People can see there's a fence and can see where they are expected to stop. But boundaries in human interaction are mostly invisible, so they usually have to be communicated *verbally* to others, not visually.

How can you create boundaries from scratch? Let's start by thinking about a recent time when you felt that someone was asking you to do something you didn't want to do or doing something to you that you didn't want. It could have been a classmate reaching into your backpack without asking you first and rummaging around to borrow a pen. It could have been an enthusiastic member of a religion with beliefs different from yours approaching you in a parking lot to try to persuade you. It could have been the person sitting behind you on an airplane, banging against the back of your seat with their knees.

Airplane seat

Let's start with the airplane seat situation. It can be hard to talk to people you don't know, especially if you're about to tell them you want them to stop hitting the back of your seat. But if you don't let them know that the knee banging is bothering you, it's likely they will keep doing it and it's likely you will have a miserable flight.

If you're traveling with a parent, you might choose to tell them about the problem, and your parent might turn around and ask the person to stop hitting the back of your seat. But if you're traveling alone or if you don't want to tell your parent, you can turn around so that the person can see and hear you and say something like "Will you please stop hitting the back of my seat? Thanks."

Even though that's presented as a request, it isn't actually a request. It's a polite way of telling the person you do not want the back of your seat banged on. That is your boundary. Most likely, the person will then stop doing it. If not, you can then tell your parents or the nearest flight attendant.

Religion persuader

How about the situation with the religious person approaching you to try to persuade you to visit his church and possibly be converted to his religion? The first question to ask yourself is where you want your "fence" to be. Is it all right with you if he approaches you and talks to you for a minute or two? If it is, is it all right with you if he continues talking to you and asks you questions about your own beliefs?

What's okay or not okay for you is 100 percent your call—but you have to communicate it! If you don't, the young man may end up persistently talking to you for over an hour and hammering you with personal questions about your beliefs. If you don't want to talk to him at all, you would need to say—as politely or bluntly as you wish—"I'm not interested," and walk by quickly. If he follows you and continues talking, you will have to build that fence even higher and say more firmly, "No. Goodbye." or "Stop."

Backpack

What about the classmate rummaging through your backpack? You could grab the backpack and pull it away from her, but that is not communicating clearly what the boundary is. Instead, try saying "Don't touch my backpack." (Whether you say please or not is up to you.) If your boundary is that others are not to touch your backpack without your permission, tell your classmate that.

Once you have let someone know a boundary exists, you need to be prepared to hold that boundary by telling the person again what the boundary is and then taking action to enforce it. In the case of the backpack, enforcing it does not mean retaliating by grabbing her backpack, but what it could mean is telling the teacher about it or simply moving your backpack where she can't reach it. The point is not to strike back but instead to take action to show you will not allow the boundary to be crossed.

Protecting Your Personal Peace

When you inform people of a boundary and then hold that boundary, it takes effort, and that might seem tiring or confrontational. But if you don't make the effort in the beginning, you will have to deal with even more discomfort later, like a six-hour flight with someone hitting the back of your seat or a religious recruiter who persuaded you to give him your phone number and is now texting you every day. The tough part will be either letting your boundary be known at the start, with few worries later, or not communicating your boundary at the start, with plenty of worries later.

As a highly sensitive person, you will probably want to be at peace and feel that all is well. Even though your initial reaction may be to ignore and avoid what's happening, speaking up to make your boundaries known is likely to protect your personal peace.

Ivy, age seventeen, said she dreaded being asked to babysit for the next-door neighbor's five-year-old son because of the loud arguments that would erupt between the husband and wife when they arrived home after going out.

The first time I babysat, his parents started yelling at each other in the kitchen when they got home from their night out, and I didn't know what to do. I thought one of them was about to storm out of the house or something, and I almost started crying. They were using curse words that I had never even heard before. But then five minutes later they were laughing, acting all lovey-dovey, like nothing had happened. It's really just too much for me, noise-wise and anger-wise. They keep asking me to babysit, though.

This is hard for Ivy because she finds both the high noise level and the harshness of the arguing to be overwhelming. She wants to earn money and enjoys taking care of the little boy, but she doesn't want to keep witnessing the emotional volatility of the situation, and it has happened nearly every time she's been there.

What are Ivy's options? She can:

avoid going back to the neighbors' house and make excuses to keep from offending them;

tell her neighbors directly she does not want to go to their house again because of their arguing;

tell her neighbors their arguing makes her uncomfortable and she will continue babysitting for them if they stop doing it in front of her;

tell her parents what happens when she babysits there and how she feels about it, letting them decide how to handle it.

How Ivy decides to handle this is up to her. But if Ivy's boundary is not sticking around when people yell at each other, she should definitely not continue to be present for the neighbors' arguments and should consider communicating to the neighbors what the issue is, either telling them herself or letting her parents do it.

How would you handle that situation? Can you think of any difficulties that might pop up later if Ivy ghosts the neighbors to avoid having to talk about the issue?

An important point to remember is that you are the strongest and best guardian of your peace. You are a sensitive person in a world that can often feel insensitive, even when other people mean well. Don't let yourself be tugged and pulled by others who don't know what it feels like to be you.

CHAPTER 6

Taking Care of Yourself

Daily life can be stressful and tiring with all the school assignments, chores at home, time set aside for friends, and rushing around to be somewhere on time. You might much rather be curled up on the sofa at home, listening to your favorite music or just relaxing in your room where it's quiet.

Everybody needs a way to de-stress and rest after a draining day. Highly sensitive people need that even more. But how do you do that if it's even stressful at home? When your environment isn't calming and soothing, you can become an expert at soothing yourself.

HOW TO SOOTHE YOURSELF AND GET YOUR PEACE BACK

You are the expert on what you need, whether it's a quiet walk in the woods down a favorite old path or a cool glass of lemonade in the kitchen after everyone else has gone to bed. Since it is through your five senses and your emotions that you get overwhelmed, these are also what you should target when you're trying to feel better.

Let's start with your *auditory sense*. When there has been too much noise and your ears need some peace, consider these options:

- Listen to your favorite calming music, whether it's soft jazz, pop ballads, folk, or ambient. You know what you like and what makes you feel that all is well. If you can't find a private place at home to listen to your chosen playlist, keep some earbuds with you so you can create your own listening environment.

- Wear noise-canceling headphones. Sometimes you may want quiet that doesn't include music or ambient sounds.

- Find a special place that is secluded and quiet, like your back porch, a carrel in the closest public library, or a bench by a creek in a nearby park.

There's nothing wrong with going by yourself somewhere to restore your peace. You can even take a close friend or family member with you, and you can each relax quietly in your own way.

What can you do to soothe your *visual sense*? When lights are too bright and there are too many screens and people passing by, try these:

- Go to some of the same places you would go to calm your auditory senses. These places are likely to be easier on the eyes and give you soothing colors or greenery to look at.

- Close your eyes and visualize what you would like to see in front of you if you could create your own environment: the mountains in autumn, a field of wildflowers.

- Neaten and declutter your environment to help you feel more at peace. If you are sitting in a room that is in disarray, with papers scattered around or clothes on the floor, you may feel anxious or negative. Take a few minutes to put the room in order and your mood may change.

- Adjust the lighting in the room. Softer, dimmer lights may create a sense of calm and relaxation for you.

What about your *sense of touch*? If you are feeling uncomfortable where you're sitting or in the outfit you're wearing, consider these:

- Change your clothes as soon as you have the chance. Choose your favorite soft pajamas or a comfy T-shirt and well-worn jeans. Kick your shoes off and go barefoot or put on your favorite socks.

- Sit in your most comfortable chair or your favorite spot on the sofa.

- Touch a soft fabric that has a texture you like.

- Take a warm shower or bath, adjusting the temperature to what makes you feel best.

When your *sense of smell* is overwhelmed and needs to be restored, try these:

- Step outside into fresh air. Stay outside as long as you need to in order to breathe freely and feel relaxed.

- Open the windows in the room, if you can.

- Sample a scent that is special to you and gives you a good feeling. Once you've walked away from the environment with the overwhelming scent, and taken some cleansing breaths, you might feel ready to spend a few moments enjoying one of your favorite lighter scents.

- Chew a piece of peppermint gum. It may distract you from feeling overpowered by the other scent. You may prefer the aroma and it may also give you a refreshing feeling that helps you cope with feeling overwhelmed.

- Wear a mask that covers your nose, if you feel comfortable doing so.

When you feel overwhelmed by *tastes* that are unpleasant or too strong, these suggestions may help:

- Take a few sips of water to help neutralize the overpowering flavor.

- Take a few bites of bread if you've eaten a strong pepper like a jalapeno or a habanero.

- Take smaller bites of whatever you're eating so that you don't experience as much flavor at once.

- Pause between bites for the same reason.

And finally, when you feel *flooded by emotion* and you can't stand the intensity, try these ideas:

- Be aware of what the emotions are.

- Say to yourself that these emotions are natural and normal and okay to have.

- Be kind to yourself by letting yourself feel them.

- Step away to get some alone time while you feel the emotions. This could mean going to a nearby restroom at school, in the mall, at the movies, or at home. You might just need a few minutes to process what you're feeling.

- Take some deep breaths. This will begin to calm your nervous system. Try inhaling for two seconds through your nose, holding your breath for three seconds, then exhaling slowly for four seconds through your mouth.

- Ground and stabilize yourself by looking around for something you can keep count of in your mind, like cars in a parking lot, bricks in a wall, or books on a shelf. Your brain will likely shift its attention to keeping track of what you're looking at and counting, and the intensity of your feelings may lessen, especially if you're feeling anger or anxiety.

Fourteen-year-old Austyn likes spending time with her great-grandmother but always struggles with sensory overload when she visits. Her granny's house is full of antique furniture with wooden chairs and thin cushions. The scent in most rooms is heavy and floral. Between the uncomfortable furniture and the strong scent, Austyn has a hard time relaxing there, and she worries her granny can tell. "Just put up with it," her mother tells her. "She's ninety-two years old." Austyn faced a dilemma. Should she play sick so she can get out of going to visit her? Should she go and just suffer through the day?

I decided to do neither of those things. My mom said it was all right to tell her the truth but in a tactful way. I told her that antiques are beautiful, but the straight backs are uncomfortable for me to sit in for more than just a few minutes, so I might sit cross-legged on the floor. I also told her the floral scent is nice but it hurts my head and makes my eyes water because I'm very sensitive to smells, so I might ask to open the windows in the room, turn on the ceiling fan, or sit out back on the patio. Granny was a little surprised but told me she doesn't mind if I need to do those things. I guess I learned sometimes it's better to be tactfully honest than to be miserable.

MAKING A SELF-SOOTHING KIT

One way to be ready for sensory and emotion overload is to create a self-soothing kit that you can keep in a box or bag in your room, car, or backpack to use when you need it.

A self-soothing kit is a collection of items that appeal to your senses. You could choose items like a piece of fabric that feels soft to the touch, a small container that holds a scent you find comforting, noise-canceling headphones or earbuds, a package of mints or chewing gum, a favorite book, a fidget toy or stress ball, or anything else that could help you soothe yourself when you're overwhelmed.

Creating the kit by choosing the bag or box and collecting all the items can be a relaxing activity in itself. You can use something you already have around the house or shop for a special item to transform into your kit. As you think about it, do you already have something in mind to put your self-soothing objects in? A blue box? A satin drawstring bag? How about objects that will help you self-soothe?

Wyatt, age eighteen, said he made a self-soothing kit in a green box from a Christmas present he had gotten last year.

I put some of the smooth rocks from my collection in there—they just feel good in my hands. I put in an old money clip that used to be my grandfather's. It makes me feel close to him. I put in a good-bye card that everybody signed at the restaurant where I worked before I left for school. When I look at it, I remember that I do have good friends and that they cared enough to get me the card. There's actually a lot of stuff I put in the box. And I didn't think I would, but I brought the box to college with me. I keep it under my bed in my dorm room, and no one knows about it.

STEPPING AWAY FROM " TOO MUCH"

No matter which of your senses is overwhelmed, feeling better often starts with the act of stepping away from the overwhelming environment. Stepping away isn't the same thing as running away or ghosting friends and family—it's taking a break in order to find your peace and balance again.

What are some scenarios when you might need to step away and how would you do it? Here are some examples:

When you're caught in the middle of loud "fun"

The pep rally Friday morning in the school gym may have started out with everyone cheering and the principal talking about the football game, but twenty minutes into it, the band is blasting the fight song, the people sitting around you are on their feet dancing and clapping, and you are feeling that you've had enough.

This would be a good time to stand up with the others and then make your way down from the bleachers to head to the restroom. You might have a teacher stop you to ask where you're going, and that's okay. You can say you're going to the restroom and leave it at that, or you can say the noise is getting to you and ask to stand or sit in the hall for a while.

The main thing to know is that you can step away from any situation—even school or public activities—where it is also okay to leave to go to the restroom. Almost every assembly, show, performance, party, dance, or meeting fits this category.

When a movie or news story is too upsetting to watch

Sometimes a movie that you've heard is so good turns out to be good but also intensely sad or tragic. And as much as you might be enjoying some of the story and enjoying spending time watching it with friends or family, the movie is just making you feel too upset inside to keep watching. Or it might be a sad story on the local news about the tragic deaths of people in a house fire, and the thought of this is so upsetting that you just can't hear or see any more of it.

It is okay at *any* time to excuse yourself from a theater or the living room. You can say that you need to go to the restroom, or you can say that you find what's on the screen too upsetting—whichever you're most comfortable with.

Don't feel that there's anything wrong with you when you don't want to view sad or disturbing content. Your heart and mind will tell you when something is just not for you, and it is being true to yourself to excuse yourself from the viewing audience when you've had enough.

When you're caught in the middle of others' drama

If you're in the school cafeteria and an argument between two of your friends starts and then gets more intense, you may find it uncomfortably loud and uncomfortably awkward to witness. Or if you're riding in the car with your parents and they get into a harsh argument with each other, you may start having negative emotions about it and feel that you'd like to exit the car.

In the first scenario, you can say "I'm heading out" or "Excuse me" and politely leave to sit somewhere else. In the second scenario, the car you're in may be moving or stopped at an intersection, and as much as you'd like to open the door and get out, you can't do it safely. In a case like this, it is good to have earbuds handy so you can listen to relaxing music or a favorite podcast or just have a way to "exit" when you can't *physically* exit.

When you feel that you're being harshly criticized or verbally attacked

Sometimes, instead of being caught in the middle of others' conflicts, you feel stuck and trapped because the other person's anger and strong criticism is focused on *you*. That's an uncomfortable spot to be in for most people, and it can feel unbearable to someone with high sensitivity.

It can hurt emotionally and flood you with feelings of shock, anger, fear, disappointment, resentment, and frustration. To sit or stand still for a verbal attack may also stir up anxiety, your brain's way of warning you that you might be in danger. You're probably not in physical danger, but your brain perceives a threat and is using anxiety to alert you to either run away and hide or lash out at the person. But you have a third option—to excuse yourself from the argument and *then* physically walk away.

Excusing yourself from an argument you don't want to be in can sound something like this:

- "We'll have to finish this later when you're calmer—I'm going to step away now."

- "I don't like being yelled at. I'm going to step away." (You can add "We can try this conversation again later" if *and only if* you're willing to do that.)

- "This is too intense for me right now. I'm going to step away."

It's better to say something like one of the statements above than to just suddenly walk away without explanation because:

it keeps you in control of you and will help you feel that you respect yourself;

it lets the other person know that you respect yourself;

it allows you to keep the situation stable and not chaotic;

it is better manners to excuse yourself rather than to suddenly walk away. (If you're afraid you're going to be physically assaulted, don't worry about manners—just get out of there!)

When *any* of your five senses are overwhelmed, stepping away (physically or with earbuds or noise-canceling headphones) may be your best option. The step-away may be for five minutes, it may be for the day, or it may be permanent.

You are the expert on you, and you have every right to take good care of yourself. But it might take some practice. Start with making your self-soothing kit, since that will help you put more thought into your individual needs!

You may wonder, *What about the people around me who are always overwhelming or upsetting me?* In chapter 7, we will dive into that topic and talk about how to cope with different types of people you may find to be difficult.

GETTING ALONG WITH PEOPLE YOU FIND DIFFICULT

Whether you go to a public school, a private school, or are homeschooled, most people you meet are going to be less sensitive than you are. You may get along just fine with most of them; even though you're sensitive, you may be a people person and pretty good at dealing with small conflicts. But there may be a few people—classmates, coworkers, family members—who hurt your feelings or irritate you repeatedly. If they don't realize the effect they have on you, they may have a nagging feeling that you don't like them. In either case, here are some common types of people who may be challenging for HSPs to spend time with.

THE EXTREME EXTROVERT

Extroverts are people who tend to be more focused on the world around them than on their private thoughts and emotions. They tend to get more and more energetic as they talk and mingle with others. Someone might be an extrovert because they *extrovert* their energy—they send it outward.

Introverts, on the other hand, tend to focus on their thoughts and feelings in their inner world and may feel drained of energy as they talk and mingle with others. They *introvert* their energy, sending it inward. Introverts often need alone time to replace the energy that got drained when they spent time mingling with other people.

HSPs are often introverts, but this is not always the case. Sometimes HSPs are extroverts. Sometimes they are in the middle with traits of both extroversion and introversion.

But when an HSP spends time around someone who is extreme in the way they extrovert their energy, it can be overwhelming. When people are extroverting their energy, they tend to talk louder, and make bigger gestures with their hands. Extroverts also say more of what they're thinking when they're thinking it; introverts may keep their thoughts to themselves and say what they're thinking only after they've rehearsed it silently.

This means that the person who strongly prefers extroverting energy could at times be hard for an HSP to be around. It may be that the person seems to talk a lot and talk louder than you would like. It may be that they try to get you to participate in an argument when you're not ready because you need time to think.

Gracie, age seventeen, sometimes dreads working a shift at the fast-food restaurant with her more clearly extroverted coworker.

> I mean...it isn't that I don't like her at all. I like her okay. It's that she's just...a lot. She talks to me the whole time we're working in the back and gets into conversations with people ordering food like she's known them for years. She asks me questions and gets mad if I don't have an answer right away. To be honest, I avoid her.

Avoidance isn't your only option. You can also approach it with a sense of humor and tell your very extroverted coworkers, friends, or family members that sometimes their high energy is too much for you and you might need to "introvert" while they "extrovert." You can also say essentially the same thing in a less humorous way if humor doesn't feel like the right tone.

Another option is to be yourself, even when the other person is asking you a lot of questions, talking for long stretches, or being loud. That means that you would listen as long as you feel comfortable, then politely step away, as you read about in chapter 6. It can also mean explaining to the more extroverted person that you need time to process your thoughts—meaning time to think about what to say—before continuing a discussion or an argument.

THE CHALLENGER

This type of person is confrontational by nature and will try to engage you to debate something you've said or to express disagreement. A challenger may have good intentions and may have no idea how upsetting the confrontations can be for you. You may at times feel ambushed by this person because the confrontations may seem to come at you out of nowhere. Their seemingly sudden "ambushes" may sound like these:

"Why didn't you text me back?"

"Why are you staring off into space and not helping us clean up?"

"Who would you vote for in the election if you could vote?"

"You always have to have a certain seat. Do you think you're special?"

"I disagree! Prove me wrong!"

Anytime you feel uncomfortable you can, of course, excuse yourself and step away. But very often a challenger respects a person who will tell them directly that they are not up for a confrontation right now. People who are very direct in their communication may want the same from you. Give them a short, direct answer, and don't overexplain. Be firm. Try this:

"Why didn't you text me back?"

I'll get back to you when I can.

"Why are you staring off into space and not helping us clean up?"

Noted. (This does not directly answer the question—it just acknowledges the complaint.)

"Who would you vote for in the election if you could vote?"

That's private.

"You always have to have a certain seat. Do you think you're special?"

No.

"I disagree! Prove me wrong!"

Feel free to disagree.

Any comeback arguing from the challenger can be met with: *I'm not gonna argue this* or *I'm not arguing about it,* or *I don't on argue on Wednesdays* (or whatever day of the week it is.) Although it may feel uncomfortable, try to look the challenger in the eye after you make your short reply.

THE CRITIC

The critic wants you to know that you could have done a better job. Critics may not be confrontational or pushy, but they can easily hurt a sensitive person's feelings when they focus on what you're doing wrong rather than giving you encouragement to do your best. The critics in your life might be teachers, friends, classmates, or parents.

In sixteen-year-old Sean's case, the critic was his father.

It got to the point that I just turned around and walked in the other direction when I saw him coming. I wasn't afraid of him or anything like that—it's just that he was always criticizing me. I was excited about my idea for my Eagle Scout project, and he shot it down. He told me why it wouldn't work. I was feeling good about my SAT score, but he told me my brother's was much higher and I would need a better score to be admitted anywhere decent. I don't want to tell him about anything in my life anymore.

Because HSPs are so attuned to their own emotions and very often also to the emotions of others, it can be especially painful to them when others don't take care to be tactful and constructive in their criticism. Sean was not just wounded by the critical comments his father made—he was also deeply wounded that his father repeatedly said things like this, knowing that they were painful to Sean.

Sometimes being emotionally sensitive is even harder for others to understand than it is for them to understand sensitivity to bright lights or loud noises, since they can see those same lights and hear those same noises, but they can't feel the emotions you're feeling.

Critics usually have no idea what the sting of their words feels like. They may know they are delivering a tough message, and they may know it will offend the other person, but they probably can't *feel* it. This is an important point. Yes, they are being critical on purpose. But no, they don't feel your pain. And that is why you should tell them. They may or may not then become gentler or more tactful, but you will be standing up for yourself and communicating with the other person instead of fleeing the scene or lashing out at them.

Imagine the critic in your life is your homeroom teacher. Student Council representatives for each homeroom are being voted on today, and you were hoping to be elected. At the end of the voting, your teacher announces another student's name, and you're disappointed. You swing back by her classroom after school when there are no students around so you can ask her how many votes you got, since you've been wondering all day if you might have come close to winning.

"No," she says, "You only got two votes. It's because you're not popular. The popular kids usually win."

You already knew that you weren't part of the popular clique, but it feels like a slap in the face when she says that you're not popular. Your first instinct is to walk quickly out of the room and go somewhere private to catch your breath or cry, but you decide instead to respond to what she said.

"Mrs. Ferguson," you say respectfully, "you probably didn't mean to hurt my feelings, but what you said really did hurt."

Mrs. Ferguson may apologize and say she just wanted you to be realistic. She may not apologize and still say that she just wanted you to be realistic. She might tell you that you need to toughen up and not be so sensitive.

But no matter what she says, you've let her know what she said hurt you. That is what you would do if she had accidentally closed your hand in her classroom door. You wouldn't pretend that nothing had happened.

You may not need to make the effort to inform the person your feelings are hurt if they are someone you'll probably never see again, like a checkout clerk in the supermarket. But if the critic is your father or your teacher or someone who is in your life regularly, the best chance you have of getting the critic to be more tactful is to let them know how their words affect you.

After talking to his therapist, Sean changed his mind about avoiding discussing important topics with his father.

I thought about it and decided just to at least try one time to get him to understand me. My sister and I rehearsed the conversation a couple of times, and then I went for it one morning when he was sitting on the back porch drinking coffee. I asked if I could sit down and talk to him about something, and he said yes. Then I took a giant breath and started telling him about being an HSP and the easy and hard parts about it. I told him that sometimes I feel he shoots down anything I tell him about and it makes me not want to talk to him about my life. He stared at me like I had two heads, but he did listen. He said he was only trying to help by raising concerns about my plans when they didn't seem solid. It was pretty awkward. We sat there for a while and didn't say anything else. The next day, though, I tried telling him about my history research paper idea, and he said, "That sounds interesting." I know he's making an effort.

THE EMBARRASSER

The embarrasser was just kidding or just curious when he asked you whether that's a pimple on your chin. The embarrasser didn't mean to upset you when she pointed out that you're chewing with your mouth open at lunch. The embarrasser was just trying to get a reaction from you when he flicks the lights off and on rapidly and asks if you're going to have a meltdown.

Most of your classmates probably find the embarrasser annoying, though you may have feelings about the embarrasser that are more negative than that. It's one thing to put up with a little teasing but this person is intentionally trying to fluster you. What can you do about it?

You have options, depending on who the person is and how much energy you want to spend dealing with it.

- You can talk with someone you trust, like the school counselor, your own therapist, your parent, or a close friend to get advice on what to do, and then combine that advice with your own sense of what will work for you.

- You can deal with the embarrasser the way you deal with the challenger—keep it short and to the point and say the behavior is unacceptable and you want them to stop. (This doesn't guarantee the person will stop, but at least you will have asserted yourself and increased your self-respect.)

- You can ignore the embarrasser. To take this approach, you will need to act unbothered. That means you don't go to the extreme of pretending the person is invisible, but you do go about your business as if what the embarrasser is doing is unimportant and not interesting enough for you to dwell on.

- You can use humor to show that you're unbothered and to keep yourself from feeling intensely negative in the moment. What's funny about the embarrasser flicking the lights off and on rapidly and asking if you're going to have a meltdown? You could smile and say, "Kinda looks like *you're* having a meltdown," or whatever comment fits with your sense of humor. If the embarrasser points out a pimple on your chin, you could say, deadpan, "I was hoping you'd notice."

Note that there is a difference between dealing with an embarrasser and dealing with a full-on bully. Sometimes there is a blurry line between the two, and teasing can sometimes be considered a form of bullying when the intent is to humiliate you or demonstrate dominance over you. When the person has malicious intentions and wants to see you get upset, then you're dealing with a bully. In that case, go to a teacher or school counselor if it's happening at school, and also tell your parents. If it's happening elsewhere, tell the appropriate adult in charge, and also tell your parents.

THE ENTHUSIAST

The enthusiast means well and just wants you to smile and have fun. This person is excited for you to come join in whatever activity is going on around you and does not want to take no for an answer. Often this person believes that you're shy, and that if they can cure you of your shyness by getting you involved in a fun group activity, you'll be so much happier.

The problem is that as an HSP, you may or may not be shy, and even if you are, you don't need to be cured of it! If you don't want to join the group activity going on, you likely have a good reason.

Nicholas, age fifteen, said he still goes to his church youth group social activities but actually hid in the bathroom last time to avoid being pulled into the group games being played.

> I saw Heidi coming toward me, so I bolted for the bathroom. I know she thinks she's helping me come out of my shell, but I was not going to join the musical chairs game. I really hate that game. You have to shove someone else out of the way or be shoved out of the way, and I'm not doing either. And there are constant stops and starts with the music. Nope, not my thing.

Heidi and other enthusiasts may want to make sure everyone is included, and no one is sitting alone, feeling unwanted. What they don't understand is that some people—very often HSPs—feel fine sitting alone or on the sidelines watching. There can be many reasons an HSP might prefer to stay on the sidelines: noise, yelling, chaotic atmosphere, laughing at "losers," gloating by "winners," pressure to perform in the game, unclear game rules, among others.

Sometimes enthusiasts urge HSPs to get involved in activities that aren't games; for example, karaoke, riding a rollercoaster, walking through a haunted house attraction on Halloween, or laser tag. Of all the types of people HSPs may find difficult to spend time with, the enthusiasts are ones most likely to understand your needs and preferences. That's because enthusiasts have your well-being and enjoyment as their goal, so they already care how you feel. They may have a hard time believing you are happier not participating in the activity, but they are likely to believe you and stop trying to persuade you once you firmly explain what you prefer. It will help if you let them know you appreciate what they were trying to do, since they may feel hurt or disappointed if they think they've failed in their efforts.

WHY ARE SOME PEOPLE SO DIFFICULT?

Typically, they're actually not. And you're not difficult, either. It's just that people can have very different temperaments and personalities. They may come from families where the household rules are different and what is considered fun or not fun is also different.

Speaking of families and households, you most likely feel that because yours is familiar and is what you're used to, you're most comfortable there compared to other places you could visit and stay overnight. So what happens when you have to stay in someone else's home or travel to an unfamiliar place? In chapter 8, we'll address that question and talk about ways to cope away from home.

CHAPTER 8

BEING AWAY FROM HOME

Because it's the place most familiar to you, you're likely comfortable at home. It's the place where you have your own belongings, the place where you can walk around in your pajamas, and the place where family members know each other's quirks and habits. You have a room, either your own or shared, where you sleep on your bed, with your pillow, at the right temperature. That's why home, even though it may not be perfect, is usually a haven. For an HSP, that may be especially true.

For most of your life so far, you have gone out into the neighborhood and the community for school, shopping, lessons, socializing, and more, returning home at the end of the day. Home has been your home base. Now that you're in your teens, though, you may be staying away from home base for longer stretches.

STAYING OVERNIGHT AT A FRIEND'S HOUSE

Do you remember the first time you spent the night in someone else's home? You may have noticed that things were a little different there: different furniture, different food in the refrigerator, different pets.

You might have had even more of an adjustment to make once you noticed how this other family talked to each other and went about their household chores. The way they had breakfast might have surprised you—standing up at the kitchen counter in pajamas and bathrobes while everyone talked about the day ahead, or sitting down formally at the dining table fully dressed for the day. Did they go their separate ways on a Saturday morning without communicating about it? Or did they plan their weekend in detail with all the activities on a big whiteboard in the kitchen?

When you start spending enough time away from home overnight, you learn that other people have different ways of doing things and that you sometimes have to adjust to that. But it can be hard.

Seventeen-year-old Paulina said she nearly had an anxiety attack the first time she spent the night with her best friend, when they were both in middle school.

It was a weird experience for me, to be honest. We had dinner on trays while sitting in the family room, which I had never done, since we eat at the dining table. Her mom let us watch TV during dinner, and it was turned up pretty loud. She let us have our phones out too. And then after dinner some kind of argument broke out between my friend's brothers. It got heated. At some point, they had taken off their shoes and were throwing them, and her dad got mad and started cursing. It made me super uncomfortable. Later that night they just acted like everything was fine and it never happened.

Sleeping over at a friend's house or even just visiting them for the day might be hard for an HSP, though it can help to know what to expect. When you accept an invitation to stay overnight, here are some ways to prepare mentally:

- Know that every family and household is unique and is in a way like its own culture or country. You may feel anxious when you first arrive because of the unfamiliar surroundings and because of being in close quarters with people you don't know well. (It's one thing to know a friend's family because you've said hello to them in passing and another thing to be around them in their home.)

• Be prepared that the household may be a lot less—or more—structured than yours. For example, you may be used to your parents making lists, making plans, starting meals at certain times, and always having a task to do. On the other hand, you may be used to having lots of free time, getting chores done whenever you get around to it, leaving plans open for spontaneous fun, and being able to come and go as you please.

• You might find their house to be colder or warmer than you would like it to be. It's possible you'd be able to ask your friend or your friend's parents to adjust the thermostat, but it will be important to think about whether the family would be okay with the temperature change. Start by asking your friend's opinion of whether to ask for an adjustment or just tolerate it for the brief time you're there.

• You might be served food that you've never tried before or that you already know you don't like. With the exception of eating food you're allergic to, it is a good idea to try at least a small portion of food that you're served. Your friend's parents may ask you ahead of time whether you like or don't like a certain food, and if they do, it is okay to answer truthfully. It's also okay to say that you have a hard time with spicy food (if you do), and to apologize in advance if you don't eat much of a spicy dish they serve. At any time during a meal, it is also okay to apologize for not eating a full portion, for whatever reason. They will probably understand about flavor sensitivity. Just don't let them think they are terrible cooks!

- When you turn in and get situated in the guest room or your friend's room (or wherever you're sleeping) you may find that your friend's family likes to have more lights on (hall lights, bathroom lights, night-lights) than you do, or you may find that they prefer to have the house be darker overnight. This is something you could ask your friend about in advance. If it's going to be darker than you're comfortable with, you can ask your friend if it's all right to plug in a small night-light near the area where you're sleeping. If it's going to be brighter than you would like, you can ask if it's possible to turn down or turn out one of the lights near where you'll be.

No matter what the culture of your friend's household is, it is okay to ask your friend or your friend's parents what the plans are or what you should do when you're not sure what to do.

Here are some other questions it's okay to ask:

Do you have some aspirin? (You can ask about any other other-the-counter medicine you have at home in case of headache or stomach problems.)

What time is dinner? / What time should I be ready for dinner? / What time will dinner probably be? (Use whatever version seems to fit that family's style.)

May I have an extra blanket?

Could we watch a different movie? Horror movies leave me seriously scared for days!

Paulina said she stayed overnight at her friend's house many more times during middle school and soon got used to the very different family culture.

I think it helped me get ready to handle chorus camp when I got to high school. By the time I had to spend a week away from home with thirty people, I was able to do it. I was used to really loud behavior and to not having privacy. I was glad to get home when it was over, but I was proud of myself for brushing my teeth in front of the other girls and tolerating the way they would all stay up past midnight talking. I'm pretty much ready to deal with any situation now.

GOING ON VACATION WITH A FRIEND'S FAMILY

This situation is very similar to staying overnight at a friend's house except it will usually be for several nights and you will be traveling, which can present its own set of challenges for an HSP. Whether the travel will be by car, airplane, RV, or train, there are things you can do to be prepared.

By car:

- You might have plenty of room, but there's always the chance you, your friend, their siblings, and possibly a large dog may be sharing space. If you have to ride in a crowded car, make the best of it by having earbuds ready, your phone charged, water bottles, snacks, and a determination to stay in the best mood possible.

- If you become so physically uncomfortable that you feel you can't stand it, try to stop and think what exactly is making you the most uncomfortable. It's okay to tell your friend or their parents that you're having a tough time, but it's better to have a specific request in mind. For example, the problem may be the temperature (too hot, too cold), the tightness of the squeeze in the back seat between you and the other passengers, the loudness of the music, or the glare of the sun on the windshield. Some of these issues can be helped by the stops along the way on the trip when you can get out of the vehicle and walk around or visit the restroom.

- If you have a tendency to get motion sickness from riding in cars, see if your parents will give you some medication to take for that, just in case.

- Check the route in advance so you know how many hours away the destination is, and you have an approximate idea of how long you'll be on the road. That way, you won't wonder, and you won't have to ask, "Are we there yet?"

By airplane:

- If you've flown before with your own family, you already have an idea of what to expect at the airport when it comes to checking your bags, going through security, and waiting at the gate. You may feel at ease about what it will be like to board the plane, pass the time on the flight, and wait your turn to get off the plane.

- If you've never flown before and your first time is with your friend's family, you should ask your parents to fully explain to you what to expect. Your parents know you have sensory concerns when you travel and know you may be feeling anxious, so be sure to bring up every worry you have to them. You might even want to make a list of concerns so that you can feel more relaxed about the trip.

- Your friend's family will probably want to arrive at the airport two hours or more before the flight is scheduled to take off, so be ready to leave with that in mind.

- You will likely be around crowds of people in the airport, especially in the security-check line. This may be overwhelming and psychologically uncomfortable, or you may be able to handle it just fine. Just be prepared to see lots of different people of every age and background.

- Once you're seated on the plane, you can put in your earbuds and listen to music or a podcast. You can nap. On some flights, you can watch a movie.

- You may feel hesitant to use the restroom on the plane, but most everyone will need to get up and use the restroom at some point if the flight is more than a few hours, so don't worry that people are staring at you or wondering why you're getting up. The restroom will look different from any bathroom you've seen in someone's house, at school, or in a restaurant. Airplane bathrooms are definitely small, only large enough for one person to comfortably be inside, but you will have privacy, and the door locks.

- If at any time you feel extremely anxious while you're on the plane, you can tell your friend, but it's most important that you or your friend let the parents know.

STAYING IN A HOTEL OR VACATION RENTAL WITH YOUR FRIEND'S FAMILY

This will be a lot like staying with your friend's family in their home, except it will be a space they also have to get used to.

- You may have some similar needs such as an extra blanket, too much or too little light, or an uncomfortable temperature, but plan ahead before the trip and bring items that may help you be more comfortable. You can bring a small travel fan if you're concerned the sleeping temperature may be too warm.

- Think through and imagine in advance what it might be like if you end up with the bed you didn't want in the room you didn't prefer. If you feel the difficult emotions in advance and rehearse how you'd cope with them, you are less likely to be ambushed by those emotions on the trip.

- Bring your self-soothing kit!

GOING TO SLEEPAWAY CAMP

You may already be an experienced sleepaway camper and know how to handle all the camp situations you'd typically encounter. But if you haven't yet gone to a summer camp where you stay for a week or so without your parents, you may have a better time there if you know what to expect and how to problem solve.

- There is not much privacy at camp. You may be sleeping and hanging out in a cabin, which may literally be a small wooden house with single beds or may be more like a barracks with rows of single beds for ten or more people. There may be bunk beds.

- Camp is a great place for making friends because you'd be spending so much time with other teens your age. That's one positive thing about having so little privacy—it's hard to shut yourself away from others, so you're likely to get to know your fellow campers.

- If you're used to having lots of alone time and lots of quiet time, you may have difficulty getting used to the camp environment. But that doesn't mean you *can't* get used to it.

- There may be flying insects at camp, like mosquitoes and gnats. Take insect repellent; it will help a lot.

- You might feel homesick for the first few days. It's understandable—you're in an unfamiliar place out in the woods or in the country. You might not know any of the other campers when you arrive. Hang in there, and trust that your emotions will begin to change soon. It's normal for the brain to stir up anxiety when it detects unfamiliar surroundings. Once your brain determines you're not in danger, the anxiety will start to lessen.

- With so many teenagers in one place, there will probably be some conflict and incidents of people not getting along. You may see some of the types of people we talked about in the previous chapter, especially embarrassers and enthusiasts. If you have trouble getting along with some of the other campers or find yourself caught in camp friend–group drama, remember you can use the excuse-yourself-and-step-away tactic. You can also talk with a camp counselor or other adult about it.

- This is another opportunity to bring and use your self-soothing kit!

GOING ON A SCHOOL TRIP

Can riding on a school bus for hours in the interstate be fun? Yes, it can. Can it also be difficult because the bus seats aren't very comfortable and there's no privacy? Yes. But you can still enjoy the trip and whatever event you're going to see or do.

- This is another situation where it may help to know in advance how long you'll be on the road and whether there will be stops along the way.

- It's also important to bring items that will make the trip better for you. In addition to your self-soothing kit, you may want to bring water, snacks, a comfy pillow, earbuds, noise-canceling headphones, a book to read, and sunglasses.

- You may be able to sit with a close friend all the way there and all the way back, but if not, try to make the best of having to sit with someone who was not your first choice.

- If it's an overnight trip, apply the same guidelines that you would for the hotel or vacation rental with your friend's family.

Come prepared, be as agreeable as you can, rehearse in advance how to handle disappointment, and tell an adult immediately if there's a serious problem.

GOING OFF TO COLLEGE

When the time comes to start college, you might decide to live at home and commute to campus, or you might decide to live on campus in a dorm or apartment. If you choose to go off to college and live on campus, it could be a new and rewarding experience. But because you're highly sensitive, you're likely to have some adjustments to make.

- Homesickness the first few weeks of living on campus is normal. As excited as you may have been to start college and experience campus life, you might feel overwhelmed by being in so many different new situations at once: new living space, new people living in your space, new geographic location, new potential friendships, new academic formats and expectations, new rules of conduct, new ways of having meal, and a new sleeping atmosphere. You might be excited about all this *and* anxious about all this, and that may give you an uneasy feeling. But homesickness tends to fade away week by week, so it will be wise to hang in there while it fades.

- If you'll be living in a traditional dorm, you might be sharing a room with another person and sharing a bathroom with twenty or more people who live in your hall. If you've shared a room with a sibling, you may already have an idea of what having a dorm roommate will be like. More about that below. If you'll be living in a student apartment, you might have your own bedroom and possibly your own bathroom. Most likely you'll have two or three suitemates, and you'll share a common kitchen and living room.

- Living with roommates is a major part of any college experience and can be a lot of fun. It can also be challenging at times since your roommate or roommates most likely have likes and dislikes different from yours, as well as habits that are different from yours. This would be true even if your roommate turned out to also be an HSP!

    - Sometimes a first-year student has a good friend who is going to the same college, and they agree to be roommates. But even when two people already know each other, they may still run into problems getting along, since being hometown friends and classmates is not same thing as living together.

    - An important question is whether you should tell your roommate or potential roommate about your high sensitivity. Although you would normally keep it private or share it based on your comfort level with the person and the situation, when it comes to telling the person you're about to move in with, the answer is yes. You should definitely make it known, though you might need to explain what it means to be an HSP and what your individual preferences are. If you explain it and give examples of what works for you and doesn't work for you, you and your roommate can have an honest conversation about living together. It may turn out that your roommate also has some particular needs and preferences.

• Should you request to live alone on campus, since you have such strong preferences? Maybe. In some cases, a student can live alone after making the request and applying for a single room. It depends on the policies of the college, and you can ask about it, if you're interested in doing that. But in many ways, it is good for a first-year college student— especially an HSP—to accept the challenge of getting better and better at working things out with other people.

CHAPTER 9

ADDITIONAL TYPES OF HIGH SENSITIVITY

Since we know that the brains of HSPs work differently than the brains of people in the general population, could there be a connection between your type of sensitivity and other types of brain differences? That is a very good question and one that lots of people are asking.

Let's take a look at some most-talked-about "Are HSPs also...?" areas.

AUTISM SPECTRUM DISORDERS

Does being an HSP mean you're on the autism spectrum? Maybe. But not necessarily. Traits of high sensitivity and traits of autism do have some overlap, but they are not the same thing.

High sensitivity is a temperament, the biological behavioral traits that make you unique. Autism is more than a temperament. Autism is formally called autism spectrum disorder (ASD) and is a neurodevelopmental disorder that often comes with social communication struggles, limited interests, and repetitive behaviors (American Psychiatric Association 2013). ASD affects lots of areas of daily functioning and may require accommodations in school—like an Individualized Education Plan (IEP) or a 504 Plan—and in the workplace.

Let's look at what high sensitivity and ASD have in common and how they differ:

- Both high sensitivity and ASD are biologically based, but ASD is considered a diagnosable disorder. ASD affects a wider scope of daily functioning than high sensitivity does.

- High sensitivity is an accurate description of up to 20 percent of the population, while ASD is diagnosed in 2 to 3 percent of the population. (That makes sense because high sensitivity is a temperament and not a diagnosable disorder.)

- Both HSPs and people with ASD can also be overwhelmed by strong emotions and have limits to how much emotional intensity they feel they can handle.

- Those with ASD may have trouble reading body language and facial expressions or may interpret these things differently. HSPs don't necessarily have challenges interpreting social behavior.

- Both people with high sensitivity and ASD may get overwhelmed by sounds, textures, lighting, or smells. Stressful environments can feel like too much, and both HSPs and people with ASD can have intense responses to sensory overload, feeling anxious or irritable. HSPs may be able to feel emotionally and physically restored and refreshed if they can step away from the overstimulating environment, but a person with ASD may need more additional support to feel better and may have a more complicated reaction to being overwhelmed.

- Both high sensitivity and ASD may enable a person to notice subtle things going on around them that others miss, but people with ASD may focus on those subtle things, whereas HSPs tend to move on to the next thing more quickly.

- Both HSPs and those with ASD have brain differences compared to the general population. Brain imaging research has shown a connection between high sensitivity and busier activity in brain regions that handle depth of processing (Acevedo et al. 2014). That means you may take longer than other people to process the information coming in through your five senses. Brain imaging research has also shown that ASD is associated with depth of processing *and* with a lot more information coming in from the five senses all at once (Patil and Kaple 2023).

Experts on the subject of HSPs don't all agree on how much overlap there is between high sensitivity and autism. Research is still being done to get a clearer picture of the differences and similarities.

To sum up, you're a highly sensitive person but this doesn't mean you also have autism spectrum disorder (Samson 2021; Rampelli 2022). ASD and HSP are separate neurological differences that have some overlap and a lot of key differences. Ask your pediatrician or your therapist if you'd like to be tested for ASD.

PICKY EATING AND ARFID

If you're particular about what foods you eat because of sensitivity to strong flavor, texture, or just the way you feel about what's on the plate in front of you, you may have been labeled a picky eater from the time you were in your high chair.

Picky eating is very often a trait of high sensitivity, but sometimes the pickiness is more than just that. Sometimes it can be a strong rejection of all but just a few foods, with acceptable foods having only a mild flavor and being just right in texture, appearance, and smell. When a child (or adult) has that many restrictions on what can be on the menu and when trying even a few bites of other foods leads to gagging, the extreme pickiness may actually be avoidant restrictive food intake disorder (ARFID; Zickgraf et al. 2022). The idea is that some people *avoid* eating and *restrict* what they're willing to eat.

ARFID became an officially recognized disorder in 2013 in the DSM-5 (American Psychiatric Association 2013), with doctors and psychologists considering it an eating disorder. In addition to the very short list of foods a person with ARFID is willing to eat, there's also a lack of interest in food or even a fear of food. Sometimes there's also a fear of swallowing food. This rises to the level of an eating disorder because the symptoms cause a disruption in daily life and are harmful to the person's health.

So if you're a highly sensitive person who says "No thank you" to a long list of foods because of flavor, texture, appearance, and smell, does that mean you have ARFID? Probably not, unless you have the additional symptoms detailed above.

Bella, age thirteen, said she was startled when her pediatrician said she might have ARFID.

My mother told my doctor I was super picky about food, and the doctor told me it sounded like an eating disorder called ARFID. I was confused about it and when we got home, I told my mom I actually love food and love to eat—I just don't like spicy, hot stuff. We went back and talked to my doctor again, and we went over the list of ARFID symptoms. The doctor decided I don't have ARFID, but I might be something called a highly sensitive person.

If you're not sure whether you have ARFID, talk to your parents and your pediatrician about it.

HIGH SENSATION SEEKING

HSP pioneer and thought leader Dr. Elaine Aron has discovered that not all HSPs avoid intense stimulation that comes to them through their five senses. Dr. Aron noticed over time that some HSPs are actually drawn to high sensation seeking (HSS), enjoying the intensity of new and interesting experiences as opposed to ordinary, routine experiences. High sensation seekers may intentionally seek out music, art, movies, scents, and tastes that create instead of reduce strong stimulation.

You may be wondering how people who want more stimulation—not less—could also be considered highly sensitive. They can be both HSS and HSP because while they are sensitive to their environments and sensitive in the way they process sensations from their environment, they also enjoy the new and different experiences and want intense sensations, as long as they can go about it by thinking and reflecting first before acting.

According to Dr. Aron, traits of high sensation seekers include:

disliking or fearing being bored;

disliking waiting around for something to happen or start;

disliking staying home all weekend;

enjoying exploration of new places;

enjoying breaking out of a routine to have a new experience.

Sisters Nina, age seventeen, and Nora, age fifteen, recognized that they were both HSPs, but different kinds. Nina took the High Sensitivity Indicator quiz and scored over 100 points, and she noticed that she related to most of the behaviors described on the test.

That's me. I feel like I spend every day trying to get away from "too much." I come home from school and go straight to my room. It's quiet. Dad fixed the light in my room so that it has a dimmer. I sit on my bed with my phone turned off. I figure the friend drama can wait—it'll still be going on later when I check my texts.

But Nora said that scenario sounds sleepy.

I think Nina basically hides from everything. She hides from life. That's very...sleepy. I can't do that. I mean, I'm sensitive like she is, but I can't sit in my room all day and do yoga. I want to meet up with my friends and have fun. Not like fun as in vaping and partying but more like being at the park and knowing you're with your best friend. I like feeling really, really alive.

When asked if she sees herself as sensitive, Nora nodded.

For sure. Everybody tells me I'm too sensitive. It's because I cry at silly commercials and I cry when I play my favorite sad song. I love sad songs. Hmm...maybe I like crying. It's hard to explain. I'm like my sister, wanting things to look color coordinated and wanting to have only certain paintings on the wall. I might want to be an interior designer. Or a singer.

Nora is an example of a person with high sensitivity toward emotions and aesthetics, preferring her surroundings to have a soft, streamlined beauty. At the same time, she is excited by trying new things and visiting new places, enjoying the ups and downs of her emotions.

Both sisters are HSPs, but Nora also is high sensation seeking. What they have in common in addition to being sensitive, is that they tend to be careful thinkers and planners rather than impulsive risk-takers. Dr. Aron noted that the opposite of high sensitivity is not high sensation seeking—it's impulsiveness, especially the kind of impulsiveness that involves risk.

According to Dr. Aron, around half of HSPs are also high sensation seekers. Dr. Aron's HSP-centered website, www.hsperson.com, has a test to indicate whether you might be high sensation seeking (Aron 2023). Check it out!

ADHD

People who have ADHD can be highly sensitive people. At first glance, the HSP characteristics might not seem to fit, since ADHD symptoms don't include seeking less stimulation—it's usually just the opposite.

The ADHD brain tends not to get access to enough dopamine, the neurotransmitter that helps with motivation and the drive to start and finish tasks. When the brain doesn't have access to enough dopamine, it will try to get stimulation in other ways, including seeking new and different experiences and following where curiosity leads. That's why a person with ADHD might not get a high score on tests designed to identify HSPs.

That's what happened with seventeen-year-old Ike, and he was disappointed at first.

> When I was answering the questions I got a sinking feeling that I
> wouldn't be considered a highly sensitive person. I could tell
> when I kept seeing stuff about loud noises and bright lights—
> those things don't bother me. I feel restless a lot, like I want

something or need something, but I never know what that is. At the same time, I'm definitely sensitive, maybe even an empath. It's confusing to be diagnosed with ADHD and still know that there's something else going on with me. Maybe the high sensation seeking thing is the missing piece.

What Ike is discovering is that who he is as a person is not described by one label or really by *any* label. He is uniquely Ike, just as you are uniquely you!

CHAPTER 10

HELP WITH
DIFFICULT DAYS

Some days are just hard. Maybe you've had rough day at school, with disappointing test grades and criticism from a teacher that really hurt. Maybe you've had a bad day at home and are feeling that your parents aren't listening to you. It could even be a day when your friends seem to be excluding you and you're feeling betrayed.

You've tried thinking positively, saying to yourself, *This too shall pass.* But even though you believe tomorrow will be a better day, you're feeling terrible right now, emotionally and probably physically, too. You may feel a lump in your throat, and your chest may feel tight, with a heaviness in it. You don't want to be stuck in this miserable state until bedtime, and you'd like to get a good night's sleep.

Read on for some quick therapy-based tips to help you cope until tomorrow comes.

HELP FROM COGNITIVE BEHAVIORAL THERAPY

The word "cognitive" means having to do with thoughts. Cognitive behavioral therapy (CBT) is based on the idea that your thoughts create your reality and that the thoughts are not necessarily factual, often causing mental and emotional pain based on something that's not really true. CBT guides you to ask, "Could my *belief* about what happened be what's hurting me?"

For example, if you pass a friend in the hall at school and you smile and wave but the friend stares straight ahead, you may first feel surprised and then experience difficult emotions like anger, disappointment, or anxiety by the time you get to your math classroom.

What happened between the time you noticed he didn't wave or smile and when you took your seat in math class? You had a thought. It might have been something like *That's weird.* Then you had another thought, perhaps *Is he mad at me?* That could lead to another thought, like *He doesn't like me anymore.* From there, the thoughts could leap to *I probably did something wrong* and then *I'm probably an annoying person.* That last thought could be painful, and you might spend the entire math class sitting there, feeling hurt.

But that pain is not based on any fact—it's based on maybes and what-ifs. CBT would point you back to the only thing that *is* factual: you smiled and waved at your friend, and he didn't smile or wave back. CBT would caution you not to attach meaning to it before you have more information.

CBT also teaches that people make mistakes in their thinking. These mistakes are called cognitive distortions. These cognitive distortions are really just thoughts errors, like the ones you were having when you walked down the hall. There are several different types of thought errors:

Mind reading—assuming that you know what another person is thinking

Fortune-telling—assuming that you know what's going to happen

Catastrophizing—assuming that the worst imaginable thing will happen

Discounting the positive—assuming that positive signs and facts don't count

Either/or—assuming that the truth of a situation is one extreme or the other

Fallacy of fairness—assuming that life is supposed to always be fair

Personalization—assuming that you caused events that were not actually within your control

Let's move from the hypothetical event in the hallway to whatever has actually upset you today. Could any of these thought errors have made your situation more painful than it would have been otherwise? Consider whether you might be dealing with some tough emotions because you're imagining and then assuming what friends, family, teachers, or people you barely know are thinking about you.

Consider whether you might be feeling anxiety because you're catastrophizing and imagining that the worst possible situation is definitely going to happen. Thinking about disastrous results will nearly always bring anxiety—don't let your thoughts do that to you. Catastrophizing is a scare tactic your mind uses against itself.

Think about the possibility that you're focusing on every negative part of the situation and discounting the positive. Try coming up with a list of all the positive elements and possibilities that you've pushed out of your mind so far.

Take a look at all the thought errors on the list and see which ones may be keeping you from thinking clearly.

And lastly, consider this:

What you're *telling yourself* about what happened is causing you more pain than what actually happened.

What you're telling yourself about *you* is causing you more pain than any actual mistake you made.

Highly sensitive people may have a tendency to be hard on themselves and could make thought errors that are harshly self-blaming, as if there were a prosecutor inside their heads, condemning them. If this is what you've been doing, consider that you should also have a defense attorney inside your head, pushing back on the accusations the prosecutor is making. Remember that thoughts are not facts—they're just thoughts. When they enter your mind, notice them, understand them, but don't accept them as fact.

CBT guides you to question your thoughts, and DBT can help you cope with the pain you're feeling. Let's explore that.

HELP FROM DIALECTICAL BEHAVIOR THERAPY

Dialectical behavior therapy (DBT), created by psychologist Marsha Linehan, is based on the idea that once you believe the thoughts you're having—even though those thoughts might not be true—you'll have some tough emotions to deal with. DBT is designed to help you deal with these tough emotions.

DBT is a therapy that can help you cope with thinking and feeling two ways about an issue and letting that be okay. DBT teaches that if you try to force yourself to think and feel only one way, your feelings will be more painful to you. It sets you free to feel sad, hurt, or angry about a situation and at the same time to *also* feel that you will be all right and actually *are* all right. You accept that you are disappointed and upset while also understanding that you are in your room, listening to your favorite music, with your cat on your lap, purring warmly. You're not either upset *or* in a safe place with your cat that loves you—you are both. Both are true.

You can probably see the link between CBT and DBT, and these two therapies work well together. CBT flags either/or thinking as a thought error, and DBT helps with the pain that comes from seeing your situation in extremes. DBT guides you to look at the extremes and see some truth in both before you settle in the middle.

For example, let's go back to the hypothetical hallway situation. You walk into math class and sit down, submerged in painful emotions. You're making the CBT thought error of either/or thinking, and you're feeling you must be a person everyone dislikes because if you were a well-liked person, your friend would've waved and smiled back.

DBT would help you start by noticing what the painful emotions are. Fear? Check. Anxiety? Check. Hurt? Check. Anger that they would treat you that way? Check. Embarrassment that you waved and they rejected you? Check.

Next, DBT would have you deliberately allow those emotions rather than fighting them off. Notice them, accept them for what they are— normal human feelings. Allow them to come in like waves rolling toward the beach as if you were standing on that beach, facing the water. Let them come toward you and wash over you until you've felt them fully and they sink into the sand.

In your seat in the classroom, you're experiencing emotions that hurt and at the same time, you're taking a few deep breaths, feeling your feet on the floor, touching your thumb to each of your fingers, knowing you're safe and all is well.

Now, let's switch to where you are in your real situation today. Pause your music, stop scrolling, and sit quietly for a few moments. What emotions are present within you right now? Notice each one and tell yourself it is all right that you're feeling them. Put yourself back on that beach in your mind, facing the water. See the waves representing the emotions coming toward you, and let them come, one after the other, to wash over you. Take deep breaths, inhaling for two seconds through your nose, holding your breath for three seconds, then exhaling slowly for four seconds through your mouth, and know that even though you're upset, you are also safe, and all is well.

To build on that understanding that two things can be true at once, even if they seem to be opposites, the DBT set of skills called "improving the moment" may also help you cope with what you're going through today.

If you can't fix or change your situation right this minute, you *can* improve how you're feeling right now. Let's do it by spelling the word "improve" (Greene 2020).

I for Imagery

See in your mind the most peaceful place you can think of. Visualize that you are there and that you have everything you need for your peace, care, and safety. Imagine the exact colors that you find soothing in this space. Imagine the most soothing sounds. Imagine and visualize that nothing harmful or disruptive can disturb you there. Give this place a special name, and know that you can return to it again and again, as needed.

M for Meaning

Think about your values—the beliefs you have about what is most important in life. These are things like love, trust, loyalty, creativity, sincerity, kindness, optimism, ambition—ideas that help guide you through the ups and downs in your life. They help give your life meaning and purpose.

P for Prayer

This does not have to mean prayer in a religious sense (though it can if that fits with your beliefs). What it means is that you pause and form the words in your mind that will bring you peace, reassurance, and hope. This may be the words of a favorite quote, this may be a song lyric, or this may be a prayer to your higher power.

R for Relax

Practice the deep breathing exercises you learned in chapter 6, pausing all thoughts to simply breathe in, hold that breath, and breathe out. You could also relax by taking a shower or bath at whatever temperature feels good to you.

O for One thing in the moment

Instead of letting your mind race with lots of upsetting thoughts, focus on one task you can do right where you are—straighten the books on your bookshelf, reorganize the songs in some of your playlists, brush the fur of your cat or dog—and don't let your mind drift away from just the task at hand. If your thoughts drift to the painful things in the past or to concerns about the future, redirect them to the present moment. Do only what you're doing in the moment and think only about what you're doing in the moment. You may find that as you do that, the emotions you're feeling become less intense.

V for Vacation

You can't take off right now for the beach or the mountains, but you *can* possibly take thirty minutes or a couple of hours off. You can go for a walk. You can go to your favorite park and sit on your favorite bench, watching the squirrels run around. You can stream a movie and ask your parents not to disturb you for a while. The idea is that you can take a break from thinking about the situation that upset you. When you return from the "vacation," it's possible your emotions will be more settled and less painful.

E for Encouragement

When you're upset and focusing on the negative aspects of what happened, it's easy to forget to balance being your own critic with being your own cheerleader. Just as you should give equal time to the defense attorney when you're listening to your prosecutor, you should also give equal time to your inner cheerleader. You might have friends and family members who take the time to encourage you and lift you up, but it will help to also encourage yourself! Tell yourself that you can get through this rough day and that you can bounce back. DBT teaches that multiple things can be true at once: you are upset and feeling down but you are also able to handle those painful feelings and bounce back.

One of DBT's main ideas is that emotional pain is temporary, and you will soon feel better. You can help yourself begin to feel better by being aware of what emotions are causing you pain, allowing yourself to feel the emotions rather than fighting them, reminding yourself the pain is temporary, focusing on tasks of the here and now, and encouraging yourself.

CHAPTER II

AFFIRMATIONS FOR YOUR ENCOURAGEMENT

Speaking affirmations can help you change negative thinking patterns and reduce difficult emotions. These affirmations can lower your stress level and help you connect with your best self.

To help you access them easily, you can download them at http://www. newharbinger.com/54032, and put them in your phone or a notebook, or post them on your mirror and inside your locker.

Say these affirmations aloud as often as you can.

- *Being highly sensitive is a beautiful part of who I am.*

- *Being highly sensitive is a gift that I'm grateful for.*

- *Being highly sensitive is one of my greatest strengths.*

- *Being highly sensitive is something I enjoy.*

- *Because I'm a highly sensitive person, I can be a great leader.*

- *Because I'm a highly sensitive person, I can bring special insight to any group I participate in.*

- *Because I'm a highly sensitive person, I can be an especially supportive, loyal friend.*

- *Because I'm a highly sensitive person, I have good judgment and make good decisions.*

- *Because I'm a highly sensitive person, I am especially good at problem solving.*

- *I enjoy being who I am.*

- *I believe in my skills and abilities.*

- *I have flaws and that's okay.*

- *I am patient with myself and with others.*

- *I have compassion for myself and for others.*
- *I can stand up for myself and do it my way.*
- *All my experiences, good and bad, help me grow.*
- *I know how to comfort and soothe myself when I'm upset.*
- *I know that pain is temporary, and I can get through it.*
- *Through my ups and downs, I am safe and loved.*
- *I am surrounding myself with love.*

ONLINE RESOURCES

Child Mind Institute

https://childmind.org/article/dbt-dialectical-behavior-therapy

Dr. Elayne Daniels

https://drelaynedaniels.com/6-ways-a-highly-sensitive-persons-brain-is-different

https://drelaynedaniels.com/thriving-as-a-highly-sensitive-person

Heal Your Nervous System

https://healyournervoussystem.com/6-facts-about-highly-sensitive-people-based-on-research

HiSensitives

https://hisensitives.com

Julie Bjelland

https://www.juliebjelland.com

Peace Family Counseling

https://peacefamilycounseling.com/resources/highly-sensitive-person

Sensitive Evolution

https://sensitiveevolution.com/minimize-social-anxieties

Sensitive Refuge

https://highlysensitiverefuge.com

Simply Psychology

https://www.simplypsychology.org/cognitive-therapy.html

The Highly Sensitive Person

https://hsperson.com

Unapologetically Sensitive

https://unapologeticallysensitive.com

Understood

"What Is a 504 Plan?" https://www.understood.org/en/articles/
what-is-a-504-plan?gad=1

REFERENCES

Acevedo, B. P., E. N. Aron, A. Aron, M. Sangster, N. Collins, and L. L. Brown. 2014. "The Highly Sensitive Brain: An fMRI Study of Sensory Processing Sensitivity and Response to Others' Emotions." *Brain and Behavior* 4(4): 580–594.

American Psychiatric Association. 2013. *Diagnostic and Statistical Manual of Mental Disorders*, 5th ed. Washington, DC: American Psychiatric Association Publishing.

Aron, E. N. 2020. *The Highly Sensitive Person: How to Thrive When the World Overwhelms You*, 25th anniversary ed. New York: Citadel.

———. 2023 "Highly Sensitive High Sensation Seekers—Giving Equal Love to Both Parts." *The Highly Sensitive Person*, June 27. https://hsperson.com/highly-sensitive-high-sensation-seekers-giving-equal-love-to-both-parts.

Daniels, E. 2023. "6 Ways a Highly Sensitive Person's Brain Is Different." *Dr. Elayne Daniels* (blog), December 9. https://drelaynedaniels.com/6-ways-a-highly-sensitive-persons-brain-is-different.

Greene, P. 2020. "DBT: IMPROVE the Moment—How to Make Crises Bearable." *The Manhattan Center for Cognitive-Behavioral Therapy*, July 27. https://manhattancbt.com/dbt-improve-the-moment.

Morissette, A. 2017. "Episode 12: Conversation with Dr. Elaine Aron (video)." *YouTube*, December 12. https://www.youtube.com/watch?v=l6fXYBqw-tM.

Patil O., and M. Kaple. 2023. "Sensory Processing Differences in Individuals with Autism Spectrum Disorder: A Narrative Review of Underlying Mechanisms and Sensory-Based Interventions." *Cureus* 15(10).

Rampelli, M. 2022. "The Hysteric and the HSP." *The Journal of Medical Humanities* 44(2): 145–165.

Samson, R. 2021. "No, Being Autistic Is Not the Same as Being Highly Sensitive." *Psychology Today*, December 7. https://www.psychologytoday.com/us/blog/the-highly-sensitive-child/202112/no-being-autistic-is-not-the-same-being-highly-sensitive.

Zickgraf, H. F., E. Richard, N. L. Zucker, and G. L. Wallace. 2022. "Rigidity and Sensory Sensitivity: Independent Contributions to Selective Eating in Children, Adolescents, and Young Adults." *Journal of Clinical Child and Adolescent Psychology* 51(5): 675–687.

Lea Noring, PhD, is an Atlanta, GA-based licensed marriage and family therapist, and holds a PhD in marriage and family therapy from Northcentral University. She provides psychotherapy for families, adolescents, and adults—specializing in neurodivergence, attention-deficit/hyperactivity disorder (ADHD), issues related to highly sensitive people (HSPs), and relationship issues. She has also worked as a teacher, school administrator, ADHD coach, and special education advocate.

Did you know there are **free tools** you can download for this book?

Free tools are things like **worksheets, guided meditation exercises**, and **more** that will help you get the most out of your book.

You can download free tools for this book— whether you bought or borrowed it, in any format, from any source—from the New Harbinger website. All you need is a NewHarbinger.com account. Just use the URL provided in this book to view the free tools that are available for it. Then, click on the "download" button for the free tool you want, and follow the prompts that appear to log in to your NewHarbinger.com account and download the material.

You can also save the free tools for this book to your **Free Tools Library** so you can access them again anytime, just by logging in to your account! Just look for this button on the book's free tools page.

+ Save this to my free tools library

If you need help accessing or downloading free tools, visit **newharbinger.com/faq** or contact us at **customerservice@newharbinger.com**.